W9-BQJ-492

Inventions

AN AMAZING INVESTIGATION

Valerie Wyatt

Illustrated by
Jerzy Kolacz

Greey de Pencier Books

Juv T48. W93 1987t

Inventions

Text © 1987 Valerie Wyatt

OWL Books are published in Canada
by Greey de Pencier Books, Toronto.
OWL is a trademark
of the Young Naturalist Foundation.

No part of this book may be reproduced
or copied in any form
without written permission
from the publisher.

ISBN 0-920775-21-7

Canadian Cataloguing in Publication Data

Wyatt, Valerie
Inventions: An amazing investigation

ISBN 0-920775-21-7

1. Inventions—Juvenile literature.
I. Title.

T48.W93 1987   j608   C87-090113-3

Cover illustration
Rob Wilson, *Jerzy Kolacz*
Design
Wycliffe Smith

Manufactured in Hong Kong

Contents

Inventing

From the moment you wake up in the morning till the time you go to bed at night, you are surrounded by inventions. There are showers and hair dryers to get you looking your best, toasters to tan your breakfast bread and bicycles to wheel you to school in a hurry. There are calculators to help you with your math homework, televisions to watch when your homework's done and clocks to tell you when it's time to go to bed. Try listing the inventions you use in a day. Chances are you'll be surprised by the number.

IF YOU'RE LIKE most people, you're probably so used to the inventions around you that you don't even think of them as inventions. You take them for granted. But what would life be like if there were no inventions? Take a step back in time 10,000 years and see. . . .

BACK TO THE PAST

You wake up in the morning when it gets light. (There are no alarm clocks to jolt you awake – they weren't invented until 1847.) Instead of struggling out of bed (no beds for a few thousand years), you crawl out of a pile of skins. Your clothes are skins too; people didn't figure out how to spin wool or weave cloth for another thousand years or so. You don't need to worry about brushing your teeth. The Chinese invented toothbrushes only about the time Columbus sailed to America (1492). Electric toothbrushes didn't come along until 1961.

You're In for some surprises at breakfast. Forget about cornflakes swimming in nice cold milk. John and Will Kellogg didn't invent Kellogg's Corn Flakes until 1898, and there were no electric refrigerators to keep milk cold until the early 1900s. Breakfast 10,000 years ago is a bone left over from yesterday's kill. If you feel the need to go to the bathroom, head for the bushes. There were no flush toilets until an English poet named Sir John Harington designed and built one for himself in about 1596. Are you starting to miss the comforts of modern inventions?

Comfort is one of the reasons people long ago began to invent things. They invented bone needles and sewed clothes to keep themselves warm, then made bricks to build houses with and oil lamps to light up the dark corners. Early people also wanted easier ways of doing things. Many of the first inventions were labor-saving devices. The harness, for example, allowed people to use the pulling power of oxen and other animals instead of their own muscle power. The wheel made carrying heavy loads much easier.

5

But the main reason our early ancestors invented things was to help them survive. The first farmers, for example, discovered that they could grow more food if they loosened up the soil with a stick before they planted seeds. About 5,500 years ago, a Middle Eastern farmer invented a simple plow and tied it to an ox for more pulling power. The result: farmers could break up more ground, plant more seeds and grow more food. More food meant a better chance of survival.

One invention led to another. Once people had more food, they needed containers to store it in. So pottery was invented. To keep track of stored food, a system of weights and measures was invented, together with a counting system.

Towns sprang up and gave people another reason to invent: travel. At first they wove reeds together or dug out tree trunks to make boats and paddled along rivers between towns. Later they added sails to harness the wind. And they attached boxes to wheels to make carts. Soon wooden carts drawn by oxen were rumbling and creaking between towns. People were on the move!

CLUMPS AND SLUMPS

Inventions seem to come in clumps, followed by slumps when there are few inventions. In the years between 5000 B.C. and 2500 B.C. lots of things were invented. After that there was a slump. Some people think that slave labor might have caused this slump. After all, why bother inventing ways to grind flour or wash clothes if you have slaves to do the work for you?

A big clump of inventions started about 200 years ago and has lasted until today. Many of these are plug-in, turn-on inventions. They became possible only after new sources of power such as electric motors and small gasoline engines were invented. Before these power sources, inventors had to rely on windmills or on water mills that harnessed the power of flowing streams and waterfalls. To use this power you had to be near the water or windmill that produced it. The invention of the steam engine in 1769 was a big improvement; you could make steam power any-where by heating water. But steam engines were big and cumbersome and useless for things like cars and planes. New energy sources made new inventions possible.

New materials and new forms of communications also sped up the pace of inventions. Steel, plastics and other synthetic materials allowed for inventions that weren't possible before. Books and newspapers helped inventors find out what other inventors were doing. Later, radio, telephones, television and computers spread knowledge and information faster than ever.

Today inventors can turn to a book, make a phone call or access a computerized library to find out the latest information on a subject. They can build their inventions out of wood, nylon, fiberglass, steel or hundreds of other materials. And they can choose whatever power source – electricity, a small engine, a battery or even solar power – best suits their inventions. No wonder more inventors invent things today than ever before.

WHO INVENTED IT?

Almost everything around you – including the family pet,* the food you eat, the clothes you wear and the chair you're sitting on – has been invented. Who invented all these things?

We know who some inventors are because they took out patents for their inventions. Patents are issued by governments. They give the inventor the sole right to make money from the invention for a period of some years. If someone else tries to make, use or sell a patented invention without the inventor's permission during this time (often about 17 years), the inventor can take him or her to court.

*Yes, pets were invented. See page 70.

The first patent was awarded in Florence, Italy, in 1421. Since then patent applications have revealed the names of inventors and something about their inventions. But many inventors lived long before patents or even before writing was invented, so there is no record of them. We don't even know their names.

One of the earliest inventors we *do* know about was a Greek named Archimedes. He was born about 287 B.C. and invented several lifting devices and weapons of war, including a huge lens that could concentrate the sun's rays and was said to have burnt up ships and troops. Like many inventors, Archimedes tended

to get wrapped up in his work and forget the outside world. One day, while he was working on a tough problem, a soldier tried to interrupt him. Archimedes rudely waved him away, and the soldier became so angry that he stabbed and killed the inventor.

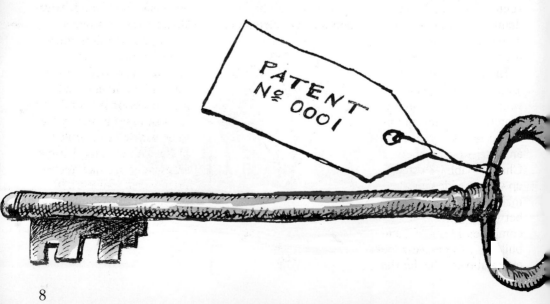

next 50 years. But in the end, his attempts failed. All he managed to do was put together part of a small model of the machine. And even that didn't work. It wasn't until 70 years after his death that inventors managed to build a computer capable of doing what Babbage had wanted his machine to do.

Some inventors have faced even greater frustrations. Just as they are about to patent their inventions, another inventor beats them to it. Elisha Gray was one such frustrated inventor. On February 14, 1876, after years of working on his invention, he began the process of applying for a patent. But he was too late. Just two hours earlier another person had patented the same invention. The other inventor was Alexander Graham Bell. The invention was the telephone.

The electric light bulb was also invented by two inventors at much the same time, in 1878 and 1879. Depending on whether you live in England or America, you might think the electric light bulb was invented by Joseph Swan or by Thomas Edison. Instead of fighting over who was first, Swan and Edison formed a partnership to manufacture their new light bulbs.

More than 100,000 inventors a year apply for patents in the United States alone. To be awarded a patent, an invention must be new (never before patented) and useful. Sometimes it's difficult to tell if an invention is useful. In most cases it merely has to be usable or possible to make. This eliminates some silly inventions like freeze-dried water. However, it doesn't eliminate *all* silly inventions.

Archimedes wasn't the only inventor to die while inventing. In 1703, the architect-inventor of a new kind of lighthouse was killed when his invention was destroyed by a storm. And Otto Lilienthal, who experimented with gliders and flying machines, died in 1896 while test-flying one of his inventions. His last words: "Sacrifices must be made." Not all inventors have made such dramatic sacrifices, but many have devoted their lives to their inventions.

Their devotion hasn't always paid off; many inventors have failed in their search for new inventions. In the 1820s, for example, an Englishman named Charles Babbage came up with the idea for a machine that was a cross between a calculator and a computer. Designing and building this machine took over Babbage's life for the

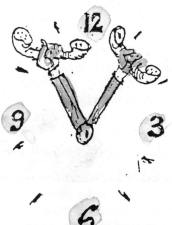

THE SILLY SIDE OF INVENTING

Over the years inventors have come up with thousands of crazy inventions including sunglasses for dogs, a coin-operated hairbrush, a dimple-maker and edible jewelry. An American speechwriter named Horace A. Knowles even came up with a device to make twiddling your thumbs easier. His thumb-twiddler has two holes – one for each thumb – so that the thumbs are kept apart and don't accidentally bump into each other as you twiddle. Mr. Knowles must have twiddled his thumbs through a lot of boring speeches to have come up with this amazing invention!

Some inventions are just plain silly. But others start out serious and get silly as they go along. In the 1940s, for example, inventors at General Electric were working on a bouncy, stretchy material that they thought might be a revolutionary new rubber substitute. It wasn't and they gave up on it. Peter Hodgson bought some of the stuff in 1947 and packaged it and sold it to toy stores. He called it Silly Putty, and 40 years later it's still selling well.

Many inventions seem pretty silly when they're first invented. For instance, people scoffed at the idea of a carriage that could move without horses pulling it. Today there are more than 240 million horseless carriages (we call

them cars) on roads all over the world. As a reminder of their origins, we still measure a car's power in horsepower.

Other inventions that have changed the world were once considered incredibly silly too. In October 1903, an astronomer named Simon Newcombe said human flight was "utterly impossible." Two months later, the Wright brothers proved him wrong. In 1825 a magazine called *The Quarterly Review* said: "What can be more palpably absurd than the prospect held out of locomotives traveling twice as fast as stagecoaches?" Fortunately, inventors haven't been put off by this kind of ridicule. They just ignored it and kept on inventing.

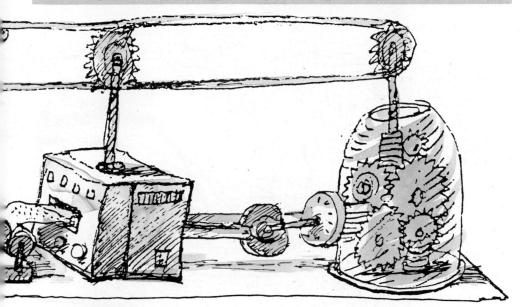

THE URGE TO INVENT

Remember the skipping rhyme "Rich man, poor man, beggar man, thief, doctor, lawyer, Indian chief"? That could be the start of a list of people who have had the urge to invent. You could add to that list United States presidents, traveling salesmen, teenagers, artists and veterinarians. Even undertakers have been known to invent things. In 1889 an American undertaker named Almon Strowger invented an automatic telephone dialing system that made operators unnecessary on local calls.

The urge to invent strikes people of all ages and nationalities. However, so far, there have been few women inventors. Perhaps this is because throughout most of history, women were not educated at all, and until recently, few have had scientific or mechanical training. Then too, there is the time problem. Inventing requires long hours of concentrated work. Most women had only short spurts of time between minding the household and raising the children. Fortunately that is changing today, and so is the nature of inventing.

For most of the history of inventing, inventors have worked alone. They have tinkered and pottered, scrounging the materials and money they needed wherever they could. In the last hundred years or so, a new kind of inventor has emerged. Instead of working alone, the new inventor is likely to work in a team. Instead of scrounging for materials and money, he or she probably works in a well-equipped company or university lab. More than three-quarters of all inventions today come from research teams in large companies or universities.

Whether they work in teams in well-stocked labs or alone in basement workrooms, inventors all share the urge to make something new and better than what already exists. Some of their inventions, such as the wheel, have changed the world; others, like the pencil eraser, simply made life a little easier for us. Large or small, world-changing or merely useful, their inventions have helped bring humankind from the Stone Age to the Space Age.

How Inventions

Suppose you wanted to invent something to make life easier – say, a self-making bed. According to a study by the U.S. government, in one year a person spends up to 25 hours and walks as far as 6 km (4 miles) making one bed. Just think of all the time and energy you'd save people if you could invent a bed that would straighten up its covers and fluff up its pillows all by itself. You've now taken the first step in inventing something. You've got an idea. But what are you going to do next?

INVENTIONS HAPPEN IN many ways – almost as many ways as there are inventors. But here are five ways that have brought success to many people.

CHAPTER TWO

Happen

WAIT FOR INSPIRATION

Many inventions come about because their inventors have a flash of inspiration, or "eureka moment." The word "eureka" comes from something that happened a long time ago in ancient Greece. The Greek mathematician Archimedes was stepping into his bath one day when, thanks to a flash of inspiration, he got the answer to a problem that had been bothering him. Archimedes was so excited by his idea that he jumped out of the bath and ran naked into the streets, yelling "Heureka! Heureka!" We've dropped the H but the meaning is still the same: "I have found it!" The eureka moment is responsible for many inventions, including Post-it™ Notes.

The story of Post-it Notes began in the 3M Corporation during the 1960s. The corporation was trying to find a superpowerful new glue, and Spence Silver was working on the project. Silver was a chemist with a playful streak. He sometimes changed chemical "recipes" he was working on, adding a bit more of this and a bit less of that, just to see what would happen. One day, while fiddling with a recipe, he ended up with the glue that wouldn't. Silver's glue looked like a real failure. It would stick two things together, but then you could pull them apart again. The problem was that people didn't want temporary glue; they wanted long-lasting glue.

No one at the company was particularly impressed with the stuff – except its inventor. He was convinced that it had a use. However, the glue had a few problems. For instance, it had no memory. When he put the glue on a piece of paper, stuck it to a desk and lifted it off again, the glue might stay on the paper or it might "forget" and stick to the desk instead. It didn't "remember" where it had been.

Silver worked on the glue for almost ten years. During that time, he managed to improve its memory, but the only way he could think of to use it didn't catch on. It was a bulletin board coated with the glue. Although the board was useful – you could stick papers to it and then remove them later – few were sold. People preferred the old-style bulletin board with tacks to hold things on.

The sometimes-it-sticks-sometimes-it-doesn't glue caught the attention of one of Silver's co-workers, Arthur Fry. It stuck in the back of his mind. One Sunday in 1974, while singing in a church choir, he kept losing his place in the songbook because his bookmarks fell out. Fry had a flash of inspiration: what if Silver's glue were stuck onto paper to make

removable bookmarks? Fry didn't shout out "Eureka!" the way Archimedes had done (and he was fully dressed at the time), but his eureka moment led to the invention of Post-it Notes. Soon these small blank notes with Silver's glue along one edge were being churned out by the millions.

Post-it Notes are used in homes, schools and offices around the world. You can write on them and stick them anywhere – on another piece of paper, on phones and fridges, even on people. Post-it Notes might have been invented without Arthur Fry's eureka moment. But sometimes a flash of inspiration is needed to work out problems. No one knows where these flashes come from. One theory, though, is that part of your mind is working away on a problem even when you're doing ordinary everyday things. Then suddenly two ideas will come together and- *eureka!*- you've got it!

WORK TOGETHER

People sometimes think of inventors as hermit-like loners in lab coats. But many things have been invented by groups of inventors working together. Teamwork allows inventors to put their heads together and brainstorm to find solutions to problems. As the old saying goes, "Two heads are better than one."

That expression certainly proved true in the case of two Americans, Leopold Godowsky and Leopold Mannes. They invented color film in 1935 after more than 15 years of working together.

The two inventors first got to know each other in high school. Both were the sons of musicians, and both wanted to be musicians. As a hobby they tinkered with photography. Since the world was in color, it seemed natural to them to find a way to capture it on film in color. They began their experiments while they were still in school.

A lot of other inventors were working on the same idea. At first people thought you would need three layers of film to produce a color picture. One layer would be yellow, another red and the third blue. Only when you put the three together, one on top of the other, would you be able to see all the colors of the rainbow. The two Leopolds tried this too, but the pictures that resulted were blurry. They thought there must be a better solution. They decided to use separate layers of chemicals on one piece of film instead of several layers of film.

The two Leopolds began experimenting. Their research so impressed the Kodak Camera Company that they were hired on and given laboratory space.

The two musicians were not what you might think of as typical inventors. For example, to time the various parts of their experiments, they sang songs. As musicians they knew how long each bit of song lasted, and it was more fun to sing than to use a clock. While onlookers (and onlisteners) at Kodak scratched their heads, Godowsky and Mannes sang and brainstormed their way to the first color film in 1935.

Today most inventions come not from solitary inventors but from large corporations and universities where teamwork is common. Some companies even make sure that every team knows what every other team is doing. That way, if a problem arises, there are lots of people who can put their minds to it. After all, if two heads are better than one, hundreds must be better still.

BORROW FROM THE PAST

Most inventions are not the work of a single individual or even a single team. They're the result of tens, sometimes hundreds of people's work over tens, hundreds or even thousands of years. Each inventor adds a new idea and builds on what has gone before. Borrowing from the past is how people learned to build modern airplanes.

Today we think of the Wright brothers as the pioneers of flight. But long before the Wrights' famous first flight on December 17, 1903, the real pioneers of flight were strapping themselves into sets of wings and throwing themselves off towers and cliffs.

One of the earliest, an Arab named Abu'l-Qasim 'Abbas bin Firnas (or 'Abbas for short), was a bit of a mad inventor. He loved music and invented a metronome to help him keep time. He built a machine that was said to produce thunder and lightning in his living room. And he conducted a number of experiments on flight. One day in 875, 'Abbas glued vulture feathers all over his body, climbed a high tower and jumped off. One onlooker claimed that 'Abbas flew quite a distance. Probably most of the distance was straight down. The flight ended in a crash. Some observers blamed the absence of a tail for his downfall.

Other fliers followed. In about the year 1000 an Iranian "flew" to his death, and a monk in England broke both his legs after a nasty landing. In most cases these early "fliers" weren't aware of each other's accomplishments. They got their inspiration from the birds. But by the mid-1800s, would-be fliers were keenly aware of who was up in the air and how others were doing it.

Some inventors believed that balloons were the way to go. One flier who thought that the future of flight lay not with balloons but with heavier-than-air craft was Otto Lilienthal. He built gliders that look a bit like today's hang gliders and made thousands of test flights in the 1890s. The longest of these flights covered 229 m (750 feet) – six times longer than Orville Wright's first powered flight

10 years later. Lilienthal was the first to realize that flying machines had to have controls to keep them flying properly. Unfortunately, like so many other early fliers, he died in a crash while testing his theories.

When the Wright brothers heard of Lilienthal's death and his experimental gliders, they began to read everything they could about human flight. They borrowed ideas from earlier inventors, added some new ideas of their own and built the first successful powered plane, aptly named the *Flyer*. As news of the *Flyer*'s historic flight on December 17, 1903, was reported in newspapers, other airplane inventors started to work. Learning

from experience and continually making design improvements, aircraft inventors (today called aeronautical engineers) have gone from ungainly planes made of fabric, wood and wire to supersonic jets, short-takeoff-and-landing planes and other modern-day marvels of flight.

But while most plane inventors were looking for new and better ways to build planes powered by engines, a few were fascinated by the idea of planes without engines, powered only by the people who flew them. Like the powered plane inventors, these human-powered airplane (HPA) designers learned from one another's successes and failures.

The early inventors of HPAs definitely had more failures than successes. HPAs usually have pedal-powered propellers. A pilot-cyclist would pedal furiously down the runway and hope to rise into the air. Then he would have to keep pedaling to keep the plane in the air. Or at least that was how things were supposed to work. In practice, few of the flimsy HPAs made it down the runway in one piece, let alone up into the air. At a French HPA competition in 1912, for example, 23 HPAs were entered and 23 never left the ground. To find a winner the competition judges had to revise the rules. Under the new rules, the HPAs had to be at least 10 cm (4 inches) off the ground during a flight covering 1 m (1 yard). Today Olympic long-jumpers "fly" many times that distance.

But eventually HPAs did get off the ground – if only for a few seconds. By the 1960s, teams of inventors in Britain and Japan were racing to build an HPA capable of winning the Kremer Prize. This prize required an HPA to fly a figure eight around an 805-m (half-mile) course. Each HPA team was keenly aware of what the others were doing. As plane after plane disintegrated on

takeoff, was blown apart by heavy winds or crumpled on landing, HPA teams borrowed not only ideas from the past, but actual bits of plane. For example, a British HPA called the *Puffin II* (so named because it looked like a puffin and because powering it involved a lot of puffin') collapsed on landing. A team in Liverpool borrowed pieces of its tail and other parts and built the *Liverpuffin*. Each HPA flew better

than the previous one, but none managed to claim the Kremer Prize.

Then in 1977 a California team headed by Paul MacCready built a fragile, see-through HPA called the *Gossamer Condor*, and a young bicyclist pedal-powered for 7 minutes and 25 seconds to win the Kremer Prize. Most HPAs looked a bit like bicycles with wings. But the *Condor* was different. It borrowed not only from other HPA

he couldn't summon up the energy, and the *Albatross* would limp along just above the waves. Worst of all, Allen's leg muscles started to cramp. Finally he decided he would have to give up. He signaled to boats nearby to help him down. But just as they were about to grab the *Albatross*, he had a surge of energy and decided to try it a bit longer. At 2 hours and 49 minutes, using every last bit of energy he had, Allen landed the *Albatross* on a French beach. He had done it!

The *Albatross's* record-breaking flight was the culmination of a flight through history that had started back with the adventurous 'Abbas in the year 875. Like many other inventions, it was the result of trial-and-error experiments by many inventors over many years. These experiments continue today. In 1987 HPA designers set a new world record for distance. A 26-year-old medical student named Glenn Tremml pedaled the HPA *Eagle* 60 km (37.3 miles) – more than 24 km (15 miles) farther than the *Albatross* had gone. So far, however, no HPA has surpassed the *Albatross's* 1979 time record of 2 hours and 49 minutes in the air.

designs but also from powered planes and even the model aircraft Paul MacCready had flown as a child. It had a horizontal "canard" wing in front of the main wing.

The MacCready team of inventors didn't stop there. They built a new HPA, the *Gossamer Albatross*, for a flight 36.2 km (22.5 miles) across the English Channel. Bryan Allen, a young California cyclist, was to have the difficult (some

said impossible) task of pedaling the *Albatross* from England to the coast of France.

Things started out well. Allen pedaled the *Albatross* to a height of 3 m (10 feet) and stayed there, pedaling comfortably. But as the minutes ticked by, he became more and more tired. Gusts of wind pushed him down toward the water and he would have to pedal even faster to make the *Albatross* rise. Sometimes

BE OBSERVANT AND CURIOUS

Lots of inventions happen simply because people notice something unusual and start thinking about it. For example, during World War II an American named Percy Spencer made magnetrons used in radar systems to detect planes and ships by beaming out microwaves and noting the reflections bounced back.

Spencer noticed that you could warm your hands by holding them close to the magnetrons. They gave off about as much heat as a large light bulb. But it wasn't until he found a melted candy in his pocket that he started to think about cooking food with microwaves. At first the microwaves weren't strong and constant enough to do much more than melt things, but by the end of the war that problem had been solved.

Spencer and his co-workers began to experiment. First they held a bag of popcorn in front of a microwave beam. The popcorn jumped around inside the bag. Then they hung a pork chop on a string in front of the microwaves. It cooked! Spencer believed it was time to put on a demonstration for his company's

board of directors. He wanted to convince them that it was possible to cook with microwaves and that the company should start manufacturing microwave ovens.

When the day of the demonstration arrived, the board members assembled around the magnetron. Spencer placed an egg on a stand where the microwaves would be concen-

trated and told the operator to turn on the microwaves. Anyone who has cooked an egg in a microwave oven knows that you must pierce the shell or the egg will explode. Spencer had probably already discovered this, but he couldn't resist using an unpierced egg. When the microwaves began – *kablam!* – the egg exploded all over the

20

Thanks to Percy Spencer's keen sense of observation and curiosity you can warm up a cup of cocoa in seconds and cook dinner in minutes. Many other inventions also owe their existence mainly to observation and curiosity. For instance, Velcro™ might never have been invented if a Swiss engineer named Georges de Mestral hadn't noticed that burrs and seeds stuck to his socks after he had been out in the woods. Using a magnifying glass, de Mestral found out how these plant hitchhikers did it. They had tiny barbs that hooked into the soft sock fabric.

De Mestral wondered if he could make a fabric fastener using the same idea. He came up with a fastener made of two strips of cloth: one strip had hundreds of tiny hooks, and the other had hundreds of tiny loops. When the two came together the hooks grabbed the loops so securely that you had to *rrrrrip!* the pieces apart. De Mestral patented his invention in 1957. Since then Velcro has been used on everything from sneakers and snowsuits to spacesuits and artificial hearts.

assembled board members. This unforgettable demonstration of the cooking power of microwaves won the board members' approval. The High Frequency Dielectric Heating Apparatus (today called a microwave oven) was patented in 1953. By the 1960s household models were popping up in homes everywhere.

WORK HARD

Few inventions happen overnight. Even something as simple as Velcro took eight years to invent. Inventors experiment, make changes and experiment again – often for years. But sometimes, no matter how hard an inventor works, his or her invention doesn't. Something is missing, and that "something" is luck.

No one put more hard work into an invention than Charles Goodyear. But without luck, all his hard work would have been useless. As a young man growing up in New England in the early 1800s, Goodyear was fascinated by the strange new substance called rubber, made from the sap of certain tropical plants. He was amazed at how you could stretch a piece of rubber and then watch it snap back to its original size.

At first a lot of other people shared Goodyear's enthusiasm. They bought the new boots and rain-coats that were being waterproofed with rubber. But rubber had problems: it became sticky in hot weather and cracked in cold. Soon people were putting their rubberized clothing in the back of the closet and leaving it there.

Charles Goodyear never lost his enthusiasm for rubber. He was determined to find a way to solve the temperature problems so that rubber could be used year-round. The main problem seemed to be not the rubber itself but the turpentine that was mixed with the rubber to soften it. Goodyear began experimenting with other softeners.

Goodyear mixed in everything he could think of – chemicals, ink, some say even soup. When a new batch of rubber was ready, he would roll it out, often with his wife's rolling pin, and wait to see what would happen. In winter, he nailed blobs of rubber to the side of the house to see if they would crack. As failure followed failure, Goodyear became poorer and poorer. At times he had to sell his children's schoolbooks to raise money. Sometimes he even did his experiments while in jail for failing to pay his debts.

Nothing seemed to work. But then he mixed in some nitric acid and the problems seemed to be solved. Goodyear patented the "acid gas" technique and sold a huge order of the "new" rubber mailbags to the U.S. government. It wasn't until the mailbags were returned sticky and limp that Goodyear realized he had failed again.

One day not long after the mailbags were returned, Goodyear accidentally dropped a blob of rubber mixed with sulfur and white lead on a hot stove. He didn't notice it until the next day. When he picked it up, he could hardly believe his eyes; the rubber felt like leather. It was soft and flexible and not sticky at all.

The accident pointed Goodyear in the right direction. It showed him that heat and chemicals were both necessary to make rubber flexible year-round. In 1844 he patented his process, later called "vulcanization" after Vulcan, the Roman god of fire.

Accidents have played a part in other inventions too. In 1878 a Procter & Gamble worker took a lunch break and forgot to turn off a machine that stirred soap. When he got back, the soap mixture was full of air bubbles and so light that it floated rather than sinking under water. Customers loved the new floating soap called Ivory, and the company was swamped with orders. Now that's what you'd call a happy accident.

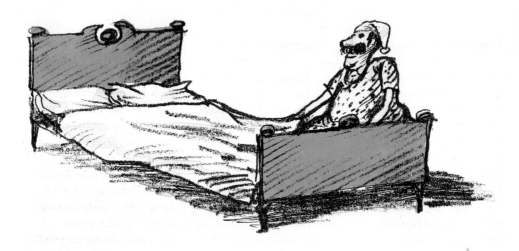

Your alarm RIIIINGS *and you vault out of bed. Time for school again! You squirm out of your pajamas and grab your jeans. Hold on... let's take a closer look at the clothes you're about to put on. You may not think of them as wearable inventions but they are, and some of them are thousands of years old.*

Wearable

PAJAMAS WITH A PAST

Let's start by looking at what you're taking off. Your pajamas have a long history. The word "pajama" comes from two ancient Persian words: *pae* meaning foot or leg, and *jamah* meaning clothing. Loose-fitting pajama-like clothes were invented by ancient Persians and Indians. But they didn't catch on right away in the rest of the world.

For a long time people in Europe wore their day clothes to bed (in winter) or nothing at all (in summer). The custom of wearing special sleeping clothes didn't start until about the 16th century. Then people started to snooze off in bedshirts or nightshirts, which were less fancy versions of their daytime shirts.

Pajamas started to appear in Europe in the 17th century, but it took another hundred years or so for them to take the place of the nightshirt. At first pajamas were only worn by men and boys. But by the early 1900s women and girls had discovered how comfortable they were and were wearing them too.

UNMENTIONABLES

Ready to put on your underwear? If your great-great-grandparents could see your underwear, they'd be scandalized. They wore long-sleeved, long-legged or long-skirted suits of underwear to keep out drafts and peeping eyes. A hundred years or so ago, well-bred ladies didn't even like to talk about you-know-whats. They preferred to call them unwhisper-ables, indescribables or unmentionables.

Underwear has been around for a long time, so long that the original inventor has been lost to history. At first archaeolo-gists (scientists who study ancient peoples) thought the Romans had invented it. But then an archaeolo-gist dug up an even older Sumerian statue of a girl wearing underpants! They think the statue – and the custom of wearing under-wear – must be at least 4,500 years old.

Over the years there have been some pretty strange "improvements" to underwear. For example, in the 1850s, women wore stiff underskirts made out of horsehair, to give their skirts a bell shape. These "crinolines" made sitting difficult and getting onto buses almost impossible. Then Amelia Jenks Bloomer invented – you guessed it – bloomers, in about 1851. She hoped that these more comfort-able pant-like garments would put an end to the crinoline, but they caught on only for sports.

Inventions

Men weren't much better off. In 1878 a German doctor named Jaeger invented the Sanitary Woolen System, which advertised the benefits of wearing wool next to the skin. Men found themselves bundled from neck to ankles in double-thick wool long johns (then called "combinations") in winter and summer. Even children didn't get off itch-free; their underwear was much like their parents'.

The invention that changed the look and feel of underwear forever was elastic, patented in 1820 by an Englishman named Thomas Hancock. He found a way to glue strips of rubber to cloth so that the cloth became stretchy. Today we call his invention elastic, because it is. It took almost a hundred years before elastic was used on underwear. Then it revolutionized the underwear industry. It meant the end of the steel ribs and tight lacing that had been used to shape women's figures. Elastic underwear held them in more naturally. And it stayed up on its own and eliminated the need for bulky buttons or laces. Thanks to Hancock's invention and later improvements, underwear is so comfortable that you probably forget about it the moment you put it on. (Unless the elastic gives out, that is.)

INDESTRUCTIBLES

Before you pull on your jeans, take a close look at them. They may be battered and stained if you've had them for a while, but they probably aren't torn or worn thin unless they're absolutely ancient. It's no accident that jeans are almost indestructible. Their inventor, Oscar Levi Strauss, designed them that way.

Strauss saw the need for a super-tough pair of pants when he arrived in California in 1849. The Gold Rush was on, and miners who spent much of their time on their knees panning for gold were forever ruining their pants. "Pants don't wear worth a hoot up in the diggins," one miner told him. "You can't get a strong enough pair to last no time." Strauss came up with the idea of making pants out of the strongest fabric around – leftover tent canvas. The miners loved them and he was flooded with orders. To fill them all, he bought heavy fabric made in Nîmes (pronounced *neem*), France. The cloth from Nîmes (de Nîmes) soon became known as denim.

The early blue jeans weren't always blue. Until 1896, they were also made in brown. And they were missing the rivets that Levi Strauss jeans have today. Those came about thanks to an absentminded miner named Alkali Ike. Alkali stuffed miners' tools into the pockets of his jeans until they ripped off. Tired of continually sewing Alkali's pockets back on, his tailor took them to a blacksmith and, as a joke, told him to hammer rivets into the corners. The rivets reinforced the pockets so well that Levi Strauss soon put them on all his jeans.

ZIP 'EM UP!

laces, he got the idea for a new kind of slide fastener. He called it a "clasp locker or unlocker for shoes." Unfortunately, like faulty modern zippers, it kept springing open in the middle. When an engineer named Sundback joined Judson, the zipper as we know it was invented, in 1906.

SHOES FOR SNEAKING OR RUNNING

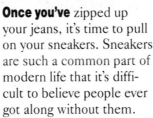

Once you've zipped up your jeans, it's time to pull on your sneakers. Sneakers are such a common part of modern life that it's difficult to believe people ever got along without them.

Long ago, the Indians of Brazil recognized the value of rubber on their feet. They didn't bother with shoes. They just let the sap of a rubber tree run into a bowl, stood in the liquid rubber sap and baked their feet dry near a fire. Presto – built-in sneakers. When the rubber wore off, they "re-soled" their feet with more rubber. Rubberized feet gave them good traction and helped to protect their feet.

When European explorers discovered rubber, a lot of people were interested in the strange stuff. In the 1700s an Englishman named Joseph Priestley used it to rub out pencil markings. Because of this, the stuff came to be called lead-eater and later, rubber. A New Yorker named Wait Webster saw possibilities in rubber too. In 1832 he patented a process for attaching rubber to the soles of shoes.

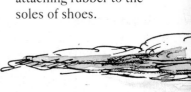

Webster's rubber-soled shoes were a brilliant idea, but they were a few years ahead of their time. It wasn't until Charles Goodyear patented his vulcanization process in 1844 that rubber could be successfully used for clothing and shoes. The first pair of sneakers were made in Connecticut in 1868.

Jeans are a snap to get into – you just pull 'em on and zip 'em up. However, jeans were around for about 20 years before the zipper was invented. So early jeans-wearers had to button up instead.

The zipper was the invention of an American named Thomas Judson. He was one of those inventors who seem to see new ideas everywhere. One day while wrestling with knotting his shoe-

At first sneakers, then called tennis shoes, were so expensive that only the rich could afford them. But gradually the price came down, and there was an explosion of new colors, designs and materials.

Bowerman had tried everything in his lab at the Nike shoe plant, but nothing seemed to work. Then one Sunday morning while eating breakfast, he spotted the family's waffle iron. He waited until his

Work on the sneaker will probably continue as long as there are people wearing them. Lately a shoe company named Kanga-ROOS has even borrowed

Perhaps the part of the sneaker that underwent the most changes was the sole. Sneaker-makers wanted the soles to give good traction and be tough so they wouldn't wear out fast. For some sneaker-makers, including Bill Bowerman, inventing the perfect sole became an obsession.

wife went to church, then took a piece of artificial rubber and pressed it in the waffle iron. Back at work on Monday, he tested the new "waffle sole." It was tough and gave lots of traction. Within a few years thousands of grateful joggers were pounding along in Nike Waffle Trainers.

a new sole design from the moon boots worn by many American astronauts. Now those should really put some bounce into your step.

MacWATERPROOF

You're finally dressed. But wait a minute – it's raining. Before you head out the door, you grab a raincoat.

Some people believe that the Spanish explorers who went to South America invented the raincoat by smearing rubber onto ordinary coats. Others say the inventor was a French engineer named François Fresneau. In 1748 he made a speech about rubber and told how he had applied it to a coat and boots to waterproof them. But the person who invented a way to waterproof cloth and began mass-producing raincoats was an Englishman named Charles Macintosh.

The first macs were great for keeping the rain off, but they weren't so terrific in other ways. For instance, if the sun came out and it got hot while you were wearing one, the rubber became soft and sticky. Sit down on the bus and you might have trouble getting up again. And then there was the rubbery smell, which might cause your fellow bus passengers to wrinkle their noses. Finally there was the bulkiness of the fabric. No matter how good the tailor, you ended up looking a bit like a walking tent. Once again, it was Charles Goodyear to the rescue.

Today most of the fabrics used in raincoats are made from chemicals. There's even synthetic rubber. But without Macintosh to start the (rubber) ball rolling, who knows how long we might have had to endure getting soaked in the rain. So next time you button up your mac, say thanks to the Mac who invented it. (Buttons, by the way, were invented thousands of years ago by some now-forgotten inventor. Until about the 17th century, they were used only for decoration or as a badge of office.)

Macintosh's waterproofing process was simple. He sandwiched a layer of rubber between two pieces of cotton. To keep the rubber soft, he mixed in a bit of turpentine. Then he handed his waterproof fabric over to a tailor, who turned it into raincoats called Macintoshes, or macs for short.

IN CASE OF EMERGENCY

It's happened to everyone. You rush out of the house, late for school, and squish off through the rain. You're moving so fast, you don't see the banana peel on the sidewalk, and before you know it – *whoops!* – you're flat on your back, feeling like a fool. But that's not all. On your way down, you heard a suspicious ripping sound. And sure enough, when you check, you see there's a big hole in the back seam of your jeans. You need a 4,000-year-old invention called the safety pin.

The ancient Greeks and Romans didn't have sidewalks or bananas or jeans, but they still had a need for a pin that could hold things together without sticking into the wearer. So someone invented the safety pin (then called the *fibula*). Some *fibulae*, longer than your hand, were used to fasten clothing together; others were worn as jewelry. Then ties and belts and buttons took over the job of fastening things, and the ancient safety pin disappeared. It didn't reappear until an American named Walter Hunt reinvented it in 1849.

WHO INVENTED CLOTHES, ANYWAY?

Some days clothes are a real nuisance. For example, you're at the ball park, caught up in the game, when someone jostles your arm and you pour a bottle of pop all over your clothes. That starts a whole chain reaction of events when you get home: someone lectures you for being a slob; you change and put your clothes in the washer; when they come out you iron them and change back into them. Wouldn't it be easier to just forget clothes? After all, skin is washable and pre-shrunk and needs no ironing. But then imagine going without clothes in winter – or in school.

That's why clothes were invented in the first place – to help people keep warm and to make things easier and more pleasant in social situations. How did clothes help in social situations? Clothes may have shown a person's rank in the group (the leader had the best furs or the fanciest hide shoes), so everyone knew who was boss. And clothes helped people attract mates – just as they do today.

No one knows who invented clothes. But we do know that he had to chase his clothes before he could put them on; the first clothes were the skins and furs of animals. Early people simply clutched these skins around them. Then, about the year 20,000 B.C.

someone put a hole in a piece of bone and the needle was invented. For the first time clothes could be stitched together, leaving the hands free to do other things. When spinning and weaving were invented in the New Stone Age, beginning in 5000 B.C., there was less need to chase after your clothes. After all, you could make them yourself.

FUTURE CLOTHES

Today you can go into any clothing store and pick out ready-made clothes in a variety of colors and sizes. This only became possible with the invention of the sewing machine in the 1850s. Several people on both sides of the Atlantic invented sewing machines at about the same time, but it was an American, Isaac Merritt Singer, who manufactured the machines, sold them door to door and became known as the father of the sewing machine. As sewing machines spread, more and more clothes could be produced. Instead of an individual tailor slowly sewing one outfit, now a factory full of workers could churn out thousands of outfits. Soon people stopped going to the tailor and went to the store.

Clothes are here to stay. But what kind of clothes? Already many of the clothes you buy are made from materials that never grew or breathed. They are made from synthetics, such as nylon, that have been invented since the 1930s. Some clothing designers are even experimenting with paper clothes, including bathing suits that are guaranteed not to disintegrate when they hit the water. But perhaps the most novel clothing idea has come from the Goodyear Tire and Rubber Company. No – they're not thinking of rubber clothes. Instead, they have recently recycled 28 plastic pop bottles to make a man's suit and tie. The material in the suit looks much like any other synthetic. If pop-bottle clothes catch on, you may never have to worry about spilling pop on your clothes again.

Edible

People have been inventing food for almost as long as they've been eating it. One of the first food inventions was cooked meat. Perhaps the inventor was a tired hunter who tripped and accidentally dropped his dinner – a chunk of wild boar – into the fire. The embers were too hot for him to remove the meat for several hours. When he finally fished the charred chunk out with the help of a stick and bit into it, he was pleasantly surprised. He was even more surprised the next day to find the meat was not going bad. Somehow cooking had kept it from spoiling.

IN ANCIENT TIMES, inventing ways to preserve foods was a top priority. After all, if you could stop meat from going bad, you could store it to eat later and spend a lot less time hunting. So people invented ways of drying, smoking and salting meat and fish to make them last longer. More recently people have come up with better ways to preserve foods.

Inventions

CANNED FOOD

You'd expect food inventions to start in the kitchen, but the story of canned food started on the battlefields of Italy.

In 1796, France's leader, Napoleon, sent 350,000 soldiers into Italy to extend France's territory. The soldiers not only had to survive the fighting; they had to survive starvation. Their only food was whatever they could take from the local farms and shops. There was no way to send food all the way from France without it spoiling.

Napoleon realized that his army could fight better on a full stomach, and when he returned to France, he offered a prize to the person who could come up with a way to keep food fresh while it was being transported.

A store-owner named Nicholas Appert had already been working on the problem. He had noticed that food spoiled less quickly if it could be kept away from air. He tried packing food into glass jars (like today's home-canning jars), sealing them and heating them to

remove the air. The result: the food stayed fresh for months. Appert's jars won Napoleon's prize, but they were heavy and expensive to produce, and the glass smashed easily. An Englishman named Bryan Donkin had a better idea.

Instead of glass jars, Donkin used tubes rolled from thin sheets of tin, sealed at both ends. By 1812, he was putting fruit, vegetables, stews and soups into these "tin cans." The cans were still expensive, so only people who really needed "food to go" bought them at first.

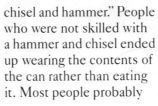

One such group was the passengers on ships. Before canned foods were available, live animals had to be taken along and fed and cleaned until they were needed as food.

Explorers also benefited from canned foods. A can of veal taken on Admiral

chisel and hammer." People who were not skilled with a hammer and chisel ended up wearing the contents of the can rather than eating it. Most people probably

Perry's 1824 expedition through the Arctic was found and opened 114 years later by museum workers. The veal was still pink and fresh!

Getting foods into cans was one thing – getting them out was another. For a long time there were no can openers. Admiral Perry's supply of cans was labeled: "Cut round on the top near to the outer edge with a

had their cans opened at the grocery store.

Seventy years or so after Donkin invented the can, some nameless hero finally invented an easy-to-use can opener.

Today in North America, can openers bite into millions of cans of fruits, vegetables, fish and meats a day. Among the most popular of all canned foods are baked beans. Eat a whole

can and you might need another food-related invention – the fartometer developed by Dr. O. Medary. Its name says it all.

Canning foods seemed to be the answer to a problem that had stumped people for thousands of years: how to preserve foods so that they could be transported. But when housewives in the 1800s opened cans of meat, they were in

THE BIG CHILL

People had used ice to preserve foods for centuries. As long as 8,000 years ago, the ancient Chinese had icehouses where they stored ice collected in cold periods. But in hot climates ice was hard to find, and even in cold climates, mild winters could disrupt supplies. Modern inventors knew that the key was ice made artificially.

Jacob Perkins, an American living in London, designed a machine that produced ice one summer night in 1834. Perkins was away from his lab at the time, so his assistants wrapped the precious ice in a blanket and took it to him by cab. But Perkins didn't follow up on his invention. Nearly forty years later an Australian named James Harrison invented an ice-making machine and built an ice-making factory. In 1873 he invited prominent people to a banquet of meat that had been frozen for half a year. It wasn't long before meat was being frozen and shipped across oceans.

Still . . . there were problems. Ice crystals that formed in the meat as it was frozen punctured the cell walls and left it mushy and tasteless when it thawed. Then, in the 1920s, Charles Birdseye visited Labrador and watched how the native people froze fish. The answer, he observed, was fast freezing. That prevented large, damaging ice crystals from forming. Using his system (and name) he began turning out small, one-household packages of meat, vegetables and other foods, which were sold in grocery stores. Fortunately home refrigerators had been invented to keep frozen food frozen once it left the store.

In recent years, inventors have come up with other ways to preserve foods. In your kitchen today, you might find foods that have been freeze-dried (coffee), stored in low-oxygen, controlled-atmosphere rooms (apples), treated with chemicals (bacon and other meats) or even bombarded with radiation (many vegetables) to keep them fresh. Thanks to modern food-storing inventions, you can eat oranges from Morocco in November, bananas from the Caribbean in December and strawberries from your own backyard in January.

for a surprise. First, the meat tasted . . .well . . .definitely un-meat-like. And it had the texture of an old shoe. The family dog might enjoy the gnaw, but the husband and kids were more likely to turn up their noses.

Inventors in England, Australia and America all began working on a better way to preserve meat – freezing it.

NEW FOODS

Have you ever been in the middle of whipping up a batch of breakfast pancakes and found that you've run out of milk? You have a choice: you can either drop everything and run to the store for some, or you can invent a new food by substituting another ingredient – yogurt perhaps. Throw in some mushed-up peaches, and presto – you've got peach yogurt pancakes. Perhaps they'll make you famous.

Some inventors *have* become famous because of the food they invented. For example, back in 1762, a gambler named John Montagu got too involved in card games to stop for meals. When he got hungry, he just slapped some meat between two pieces of bread and ate as he played. His invention was named after him. (John Montagu's formal title was the fourth Earl of Sandwich.)

Two other food inventors who became famous for their invention were John and Will Kellogg. The story of how they invented the first breakfast cereal in 1894 is a mixture of hard work and happy accident.

John Kellogg was a doctor who believed that Americans' diets were unhealthy. So he and his brother Will started a sanatorium where people could go to eat healthy meals and recover their health. John's special interest was breakfast. He believed that people should eat a light breakfast instead of the heavy, greasy foods most Americans started their days with. In his spare time he set to work making a health bread especially for breakfast.

The Kellogg brothers started experimenting with wheat in the barn behind their sanatorium. They tried everything. They boiled it, mashed it and rolled it out flat, but nothing they ended up with looked – or tasted – like bread. One failure led to another. By accident one batch of boiled wheat was left to mold in a pot. When John discovered it, something made him try rolling the moldy mush out. The result was surprising. Each grain of wheat came out as a separate flake. To dry the flakes, John browned them lightly in the oven. A few more tries and the Kelloggs were able to produce wheat flakes without the mold.

The Kelloggs gave up the search for a health bread and served their new breakfast food in the dining room of their sanatorium. Although the flakes were tough and bland, people were soon ordering bags of them to take home. The Kelloggs began experiments with corn. Four years after wheat flakes were invented, the first tray full of Kellogg's Corn Flakes came out of the oven.

In all, the Kellogg brothers invented more than 100 health foods. One of the most popular is the breakfast cereal Rice Crispies. To introduce it to the public, illustrator Vernon Grant invented three gnome-like characters called Snap, Crackle and Pop.

Not all food inventors become famous for their inventions. For example, the world has long forgotten the inventor of the chocolate sundae. It was created by a Wisconsin store-owner named Smithson in 1890. Smithson regularly ran out of ice cream on Sundays, because there were no deliveries that day. To stretch his ice cream supply, he served smaller portions and added chocolate sauce. He figured customers would be distracted by the chocolate sauce and wouldn't notice that the scoops of ice cream were smaller. The "ice cream Sundays" caught on, and soon people were asking for them on Mondays, Tuesdays – just about every day of the week. When a religious customer objected to the name, Smithson changed it from Sundays to sundaes.

CHAPTER FOUR

FUTURE FOOD

Today new food inventions hit the supermarkets every day. But food inventors haven't stopped there. They've even begun inventing the plants and animals food is made from.

If you think it sounds far-fetched for someone to "invent" a plant, you may be surprised to learn that most of the foods you eat have been invented. How? Farmers, and later scientists, selected the biggest, healthiest plants and animals and bred them with other healthy specimens. This "selective breeding" gradually produced huge pigs, slow-ripening bananas and other invented foods that show up on your plate. Today scientist-inventors are also trying to create entirely new plants and animals.

Take the pomato, for example. It's a cross between – you guessed it – a tomato and a potato. Scientists thought the pomato would make a terrific space-saver; it could produce potatoes underground and tomatoes above ground at the same time. They finally managed to grow a pomato, but it didn't produce either potatoes or tomatoes.

Some of the plants that scientist-inventors are working on today will be the super-plants of tomorrow. They'll be bigger, healthier and better at fighting off the diseases and frosts that destroy ordinary plants. But those aren't the only reasons for trying to invent new plants.

Scientist-inventors in the United States are trying to create square tomatoes, which would be much easier to stack in boxes for shipping. (They'd probably fit better on a square slice of bread too.) Other scientists are working on wheat that

can survive when watered with salt water. If they succeed, wheat can be grown in desert coastal regions where there's little fresh water but lots of salt water. One enterprising inventor, Eudora Pettigrew, has even invented a highrise greenhouse for city farming. According to her design, plants would travel up through the greenhouse on a conveyor belt, getting sun at one point and water and fertilizer at another.

Junk-food fans will be pleased to learn that healthier snacks are on the way too. In a few years you may be munching on carrots that are so sweet and crunchy that they'll take the place of candy, or on super-flavored popcorn that doesn't need salt or butter.

What about animals? Scientists recently discovered that they could combine mouse and rat cells to get rat-sized mice. Then they managed to cross a goat and a sheep. The resulting animal (some say it should be called a "geep," others a "shoat") looked like both its parents.

Through these types of experiments, scientist-inventors hope to produce bigger or even new types of animals and plants to meet the world's growing demand for food. They've already come a long way. In 1860 a farm worker could only grow enough food for five people. Today, thanks to inventions in farm machinery, fertilizers, and plant and animal breeding methods, each farm worker can produce enough food to feed 80 people.

In 1986, a group of scientists took another major step into the future. After years of experimentation, they managed to implant the genes of a firefly into a tobacco plant. The resulting plant-animal actually glows in the dark, but only very faintly. It has no use, except to give scientists more information about how genes work separately and together. Some people find the idea of a life form that's half plant and half animal quite frightening. One of this plant-animal's inventors, Stephen Howell, is reassuring: "At this time, this is only a laboratory creature. And plants don't fly or crawl across the floor or creep into mouse holes. You can set one down and be pretty sure that's where it's going to be when you look again."

Around-the-House Inventions

Put down this book for a minute and take a look around. You're sitting in the middle of a museum crammed full of inventions from all different periods of history. Some household inventions are younger than you are; others have been around almost as long as people have.

ONE OF THE oldest inventions of them all is the house itself. Long, long ago, before houses were invented, people lived in caves and other natural shelters. When they had to move – perhaps to find new hunting grounds – they built houses that looked a lot like the caves they had left behind. They would dig a shallow hole in the ground and drag branches or rocks around it to form a shelter from the wind.

OVER THOUSANDS OF years primitive shelters were replaced by huts and then by square houses made of brick, stone or wood. The ancient Greeks and Romans even used concrete to build spacious and beautiful homes with many rooms. They also invented many comforts for the home, including running water. But their inventions were lost, forgotten or destroyed when barbarian tribes took over. This takeover marked the beginning of the Dark Ages, during which homes became cold, dark, comfortless places.

FOR A LONG time, many houses in much of Europe were just one big open space with no rooms. People ate and slept around a central fire pit, and a hole in the ceiling let out the smoke. Then, in the 1200s, the weather got colder and people had to find better ways to stay warm. One of the first things they did was to stop heat from disappearing up the ceiling hole by building fireplaces to hold and radiate the heat. Big houses might have had several fireplaces, and areas around these fireplaces were closed off to help capture the heat. These enclosed areas were the first rooms.

THE INVENTION OF rooms gave people privacy for the first time. But not much of it. People had to go through one room to get to the next. Hallways, which allowed rooms to be closed off, weren't invented until later. Gradually certain rooms began to be used for sleeping, others for cooking and eating, and still others for bathing. And they became filled with many of the inventions we still use today, such as beds, televisions, stoves and toilets.

SOME HOUSEHOLD INVENTIONS have surprising histories. Let's start your own personal museum tour with one of the oldest rooms in the house – the bathroom. If you've ever been locked out of the bathroom by a brother or sister taking a long hot bath, you have some idea of how impossible it would be to live without one. The bathroom is home to three indispensable inventions – the bathtub, the sink and the toilet.

SPLISH SPLASH

A lot of inventions change over time as one inventor after another makes improvements. But not the bathtub. Bathtubs that look pretty much like yours were around in the palace of Knossos on the island of Crete (now part of Greece) almost 4,000 years ago. Then strange things started happening to the bathtub. The Romans enlarged the bathtub and made it a community meeting place. At the Baths of Caracalla in Rome, for example, you could take a bath with 1,599 other people in a series of huge bathtubs.

The Dark Ages, which followed Roman times, might just as well be called the Dirty Ages. People no longer got together in public baths; most of them never took a bath at all. It wasn't until after the year 1000 that taking baths once more came into style.

Since then, many people have tried to invent a better bathtub. "Hip" or "sitz" baths were half-sized tubs that a person sat in. There were boot-shaped baths to lounge in (the covered top of the tub was supposed to keep in heat). There have even been portable travel-ing baths. But people have always gone back to the old-style bathtubs first in-vented on Crete. One recent bathtub invention does look promising, however. It's a foot-operated faucet system that will allow bathers to add hot or cold water with the flick of a toe.

WASHING UP

The sink is a newcomer to the bathroom. It started out in the dining room and moved to the bedroom before finally ending up next to the tub and toilet.

The first sinks, actually portable basins, were invented because forks weren't. People ate with their hands from shared bowls, so it was the custom to wash up before digging in. In wealthy homes, servants would go from person to person with a basin of water before the meal started. Later, basins were fixed to walls outside the dining room.

The next place the sink turns up is the bedroom. You may have seen old basin and pitcher sets in antique shops. These were once part of the furniture of bedrooms. When you got up in the morning you poured some water into the basin and washed up. In winter, you might have to crack a layer of ice in the pitcher first. When water was piped into homes, the sink was moved into a special bathroom where it could be attached to the water supply with the other water-using appliances.

On or near your sink you'll probably find two more bathroom inventions: a bar of soap and a toothbrush. Soap was invented even before there were bathrooms – probably around 3000 B.C. But for a long time, people rarely used it. Early bathers either scrubbed themselves with an oil and sand mixture or had their servants hit them with tree branches to beat the dirt off. Soap hasn't changed much over the years, except for the invention of see-through soap, invented by Andrew Pears in 1789, and floating soap (for more about this invention, see page 23).

Toothbrushes were invented by the Chinese in the late 1400s. At first they were made out of animal hair, such as pig bristles. Finally, in 1938, the first nylon toothbrushes appeared on the market. Toothpaste had been around for years. But toothpaste in a tube wasn't invented until an American named Washington Sheffield designed a collapsible metal toothpaste tube in 1892. Not surprisingly, Dr. Sheffield was a dentist.

THE ROYAL FLUSH

If you're like most people, you hardly give the toilet a thought – until you need to use it. But over the years, hundreds of people have spent thousands of hours thinking about a clean and odorless way of disposing of human waste.

The first toilets have been found in the ruins of ancient cities. These toilets look like a Stone Age version of our own. The seats are carved stone, instead of plastic, and the waste falls into a stone pit instead of a ceramic bowl. There it would collect until someone removed it – and probably used it as fertilizer for the crops.

Later toilet-users came up with more ingenious solutions. For example, in the 13th and 14th centuries, castle toilets were positioned over moats or rivers. When they were in use, the waste would drop down into the water below — the same water that people used for drinking, cooking and washing. Some wealthy people had beautifully decorated chairs that hid a toilet seat suspended over a pan. Most people simply used chamber pots and dumped the contents out the window. It was con-

sidered courteous to warn people passing by on the sidewalk before doing this. But even so, passersby learned to step aside if an upstairs window opened.

This bad-smelling situation might have gone on for a long time had it not been for Queen Elizabeth I. She had a sensitive sense of smell and took baths much more often than most people (about once a month). Had she not been queen, people would have thought her a bit mad. Her godson Sir John Harington shocked everyone who knew him by bathing every day. To please his godmother and himself, Harington invented the first flush toilet around 1596. It was surprisingly similar to the ones we have today: when a handle was pulled, a reservoir of water flowed into a bowl and "flushed" it out. But Harington was ahead of his time. People preferred to dump rather than flush, so his toilet didn't catch on. It wasn't until 1775 that a British inventor named Alexander Cummings took out a patent for the granddaddy of our modern toilet. Joseph Bramah made improvements to Cummings's design and started manufacturing "water closets" three years later.

THE THOROUGHLY MODERN KITCHEN

Next stop on your tour is the kitchen, which probably has more inventions than any other room in the house. Just think of the inventions you use to make breakfast. You open the **fridge** and take out an orange. You squeeze a **glass** of juice on an **orange juicer.** Next you cut a piece of bread with a **knife** and pop it in the **toaster.** While it's toasting, you crack an egg into a **non-stick pan** and fry it on the **stove.** When everything is cooked, you put it all on a **plate, spoon** some jam on the toast and sit down to eat. It's not even 8 o'clock and already you've used nine inventions!

Many kitchen inventions are labor-savers. They use electric motors instead of human strength to get jobs done. For example, there are electric food processors to chop things, electric blenders and electric beaters to mix things and electric brooms to "sweep up" the mess when you're through cooking. These labor-savers were only possible after the discovery of electricity and the invention of small electric motors. Most of them weren't invented until after homes in North America and Europe were "electrified" (connected to a source of electricity) in the 20th century.

Other kitchen inventions, such as the microwave oven and toaster, are time-savers. For example, to make toast a century ago, your ancestors had to wait until the cooking fire burnt down to red-hot coals and then make sure the bread slices didn't burn. When one side was done, they had to flip the bread over and watch some more. Usually the job of watching – like the jobs of cooking and cleaning – was done by women. New time-saving and labor-saving appliances launched the "kitchen revolution" and helped to free women from much of the household drudgery.

Many kitchen appliances were invented only after electricity came into homes, but some are hundreds of years old. Plates, for example, were invented in the Middle Ages. You might expect the first plates to have been made out of pottery, but they weren't. They were made out of bread. Before a meal, bakers would whip up a batch of flat round loaves of bread. These would be sliced in half to make two plate-like disks. Diners ate from these "trenchers" the way we eat from plates. At the end of the meal, it was considered bad manners to eat your plate. That was left to the servants who got stuck with cleaning up.

Plates aren't nearly as tasty as they once were, but they do last longer. Since we can no longer eat our plates, however, it would be handy if someone invented a self-washing plate. Sound silly? Many of our modern kitchen inventions *do* manage to clean or otherwise take care of themselves. For example, there are self-defrosting fridges, self-cleaning ovens and other machines, such as microwave ovens, that refuse to work unless they're being used properly. In future there will be appliances that not only flash, beep or buzz when broken but even call the repair shop. It's enough to make you wonder who's the boss, isn't it?

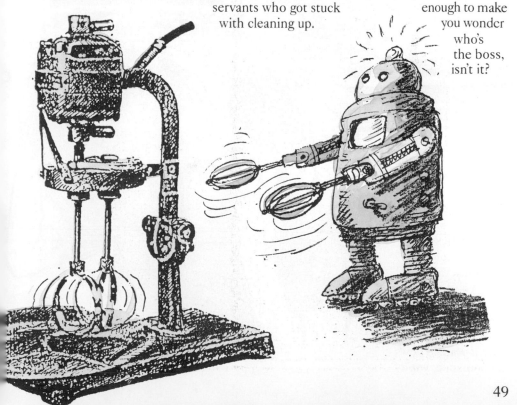

HELLO WORLD!

The next stop on our house museum tour might be called the communications center. However, you probably call it the living room. In many living rooms you'll find a record player, television and telephone, three inventions that link the home to the outside world. Life without these three inventions would be very

either have to send it by mail or deliver it in person. Finally, you'd have to find new ways to have fun, with no television or records to help you out.

Inventing ways to send sounds and (later) pictures from one place to another became an obsession for many people in the 1860s and 1870s. Several inven-

tors in Italy, Russia, Germany, the United States, Canada and Britain began working on the same ideas at the same time. One of the first to be successful was Alexander Graham Bell. He had noticed that sounds made the air vibrate. You can see this for yourself. Cut a mouth-sized hole in an empty cardboard toilet

different. First, there'd be no music, except what you made yourself. So you'd probably have to spend a lot more time practicing the piano or violin. Secondly, the only news you'd get about the world outside the home would be from newspapers. And if *you* had news for someone, you'd paper roll and stretch a piece of toilet paper over one end, using an elastic band to keep it in place. Hold the roll upright, so that the toilet-paper-covered end is up. Put a few grains of rice on the toilet paper and speak into the hole. The sound of your voice makes the air vibrate and jiggle the rice.

current that could be sent over a wire. In a receiver, the electrical quivers were turned back into vibrations.

words: "Mr. Watson, come here. I want you."

Next came the record player. Thomas Edison, who later went on to play an important role in the invention of the light bulb,

Alexander Graham Bell used this idea to invent the telephone in Brantford, Ontario, in 1874. The vibrations in the air caused by someone speaking into a mouthpiece were turned into a quivering electrical

The result sounded just like the human voice that had made the sound in the first place. Fittingly, Bell made the first phone call. His assistant, Watson, listened at the receiver in a nearby room and heard these

invented the phonograph in 1877. His phonograph could both record voices and play them back. Instead of flat records, it used waxed paper wrapped around a cylindrical drum.

A needle-like stylus both cut tiny grooves in the paper and played the sounds back later. A large horn-shaped speaker amplified the sound. The first recording ever made was Edison reciting "Mary Had a Little Lamb." In 1888, Emile Berliner improved on the phonograph by inventing the gramophone, which played flat disk records. Stereophonic records giving different sounds through right and left speakers became available only in 1958.

Alexander Graham Bell's telephone and Edison's phonograph changed the home – and the world. But some inventors had an even more revolutionary idea. They wanted to send voices and pictures from place to place without wires. Several scientists thought wireless communication was possible, but it took a young Italian named Guglielmo Marconi to take the first step.

Marconi started experimenting with electricity when he was 16 years old. At first he discovered a way to make a bell ring across the room by signaling to it over invisible radio waves in the air. Then he enlisted his brother's help to see how far his signaling would carry. His brother would carry a receiver and Marconi would send signals to it. Little by little his

brother increased the distance between himself and Marconi. Soon he was so far away that he had to wave to Marconi with a white flag to indicate that he had received the signal. Marconi knew his wireless radio was a success when he could signal to his brother's receiver even when his brother was out of sight.

But Marconi's radio wasn't like the radio you listen to today. It could only transmit signals by sending out a continuous tone and breaking it up according to a code, much as you might signal someone by flicking a flashlight on and off. It

took several changes to his idea by inventors in Britain, the United States and Canada before human voices could actually be broadcast over the radio. The first broadcast of the human voice took place on December 23, 1900. A Canadian named Reginald Aubrey Fessenden spoke these typically Canadian words over the radio to his assistant: "Is it snowing where you are, Mr. Thiessen?"

Radio was half of television – the sound part. But getting the pictures to go with it took almost 70 years of experimenting. People began to work on transmit-

ting pictures in the 1880s. They understood that a picture can be seen as an arrangement of tiny dots, each of which is dark or light or gray. The idea behind transmitting a picture was to scan it dot by dot in order, reading the brightness of each dot, and then to send this information by radio to a receiver (a television set). To put the picture together again, the process was reversed. And this whole process – turning the picture into dots, sending the information on each dot and reconstructing the dots into a picture – had to be done very, very fast.

One problem facing inventors was how to break down and send information about the picture. The first solution came from a German inventor named Paul Nipkow. In 1884 he invented a scanning disk to do the job, and a television with the Nipkow disk was demonstrated by John Logie Baird in England in 1926.

Baird's television didn't look much like the box you watch today. It was made out of bits of borrowed equipment, including a knitting needle and an old bicycle light. Nor was the picture like anything you'd see today. It was a bright pinkish color with stripes that almost hid the picture. But if you looked closely, you could make out the blurred face. Who was the first television "star"? A ventriloquist's dummy!

Despite the problems, people were amazed when pictures appeared on the screen. The big advance came when an American born in Russia, Vladimir Zworykin, developed an *electronic* scanning device in 1923. It sharpened up the picture and paved the way for our modern television.

If Alexander Graham Bell, Thomas Edison, Vladimir Zworykin and the other communication pioneers could walk into your living room, they'd be stunned by what they saw. They'd see video cassette recorders, compact disk players and other refinements to their inventions that they never dreamed would be possible. In the future – who knows? – even *you* might find the inventions in your living room a bit surprising.

CLEANING UP THE DRUDGERY

While high technology has helped to bring the outside world into your home, it hasn't done much to help with the cleaning. Someone still has to mop and dust and make beds. There have been a *few* improvements, however.

For example, there's the vacuum cleaner. In the mid-19th century, several people tried to invent a carpet cleaner that would eliminate the need to beat rugs outdoors. Many early carpet cleaners either used brushes to whisk the dirt up, as today's carpet-sweepers do, or sucked the dirt up by using a bellows-like mechanism. It took two people to work the bellows-style cleaners. One had to pump the bellows to create enough suction to suck up the dirt, while another ran the connected hose over the carpet.

When electric motors appeared, carpet cleaners changed. One electric cleaner blew air down onto the carpet and bounced the dirt up into a box. While watching a demonstration of this cleaner – which also bounced a fair amount of dirt all over the room – an Englishman named Cecil Booth had a better idea. He placed a handkerchief over his mouth, lay down on the carpet and started to suck.

(Fortunately he waited until he got home before trying this.) As he had thought, dirt was sucked up and caught in the handkerchief. In 1901 Booth succeeded in building the first vacuum cleaner, using the same idea he had tried out himself. But Booth's first vacuum cleaners weren't exactly household conveniences. They were so big they had to be towed from house to house by horses. They sat outside while long hoses snaked into nearby houses and sucked up the dirt. But they made so much noise that people complained they were spooking horses. Seven years later, in 1908, an American named James Spangler miniaturized the vacuum, and cleaning has been a lot easier ever since.

HOME SWEET HOME

The world still awaits the invention of the self-making bed, but one inventive American named Francis Gabe believes she has come up with the solution to most of our other cleaning problems. She invented a self-cleaning house in 1955 and even built one. To operate it, you simply push a

button. Instantly water and soap spray out of openings in the floor and ceiling, cleaning everything in sight. (All the furniture in the house is waterproof, including upholstery – another Gabe invention.) After the wash and a rinse, air blowers, like house-sized hair dryers, dry things off. Total cleaning time: one hour.

A self-cleaning house may sound crazy, but it looks tame compared with what some architects and inventors have in mind for the home of the future.

One German architect thinks we should be growing our own homes, and he proved it can be done. He wove together a house by intertwining the branches of some hazel trees. To keep himself warm in winter, he insulated with more plants. Now that's what you'd call a tree house.

Some inventors think we may be living in apartments plugged into a central trunk. When you wanted to move, you'd just unplug your home and plug it into a new apartment trunk. Others envision a smart house. It would be able to sense when you walked in and what lights should be turned on, and it would even let you know if a window had jammed or other problems arose.

One of the most unusual ideas is the inflatable home, complete with inflatable furniture. Going on holiday? Simply deflate your house, pack it in your suitcase and inflate it again at the other end. If someone does manage to invent an inflatable home, it will provide work for thousands of other inventors. They'll be busy trying to invent the inflatable bathtubs, fridges, stoves and televisions to go in it.

Inventions That Made a Big Difference

When Joseph Glidden, an Illinois farmer, started to twist pieces
of wire on his backyard grindstone and add spikes here and
there, no one – not even Glidden himself – knew that he was
inventing something that would change the world around him.
Glidden had invented barbed wire, and he patented it in 1874.

UP UNTIL THE invention of barbed wire, the West had been mostly
cattle country. Farmers who tried to settle and plant crops usually had a tough
time; cattle from nearby herds roamed onto their land and ate their crops.

FARMERS IMMEDIATELY SAW the usefulness of barbed-
wire fences. They were a cheap and reliable way to keep cattle off their land.
The cattle ranchers, on the other hand, weren't so pleased with the idea of
fenced-in land. They wanted their cattle to roam free. "Fence wars" broke out
between farmers and ranchers. Farmers would put up barbed-wire fences
and cattle ranchers would cut them down. In 1888, a Texas Ranger reported,
"While a man was putting up his fence one day in a hollow, a crowd of
wire-cutters was cutting it behind him in another hollow back over the hill."
But the farmers and their barbed wire had come to stay.

BARBED WIRE STARTED out small but ended up making a big
difference. By fencing in the American West, it helped to open up a whole new
territory for farming. Today grain from this farming land feeds millions of
people every year.

MANY OTHER INVENTIONS have made a big difference too.
They have changed the way people live, the way countries develop and even
the way we think. Here are the stories behind five world-changing inventions.
Some of them have surprisingly humble beginnings.

CHAPTER SIX

WRITING

With just 26 letters you can write a letter to a pen pal, complete an exam or even compose a poem – provided you have a pen or pencil, and paper, that is. Thousands of years ago, people had no way of writing things down. Instead, news, knowledge and information were passed along by word of mouth. If you've ever played the party game where one person whispers a message to the next, who whispers to the next, and so on, you know how unreliable word of mouth can be. First, like the party-game whispering, the message gets mixed up. Secondly, bits of it are forgotten. Writing things down changed all that.

The first written "language" was invented by cave dwellers who wanted to tell other people about the day's hunt. They used brushes made of bits of animal hair tied together to paint pictures on the cave walls of themselves and the animals they had killed.

Eventually several writing systems were invented, including Chinese characters and hieroglyphs in Egypt. These led to the invention of an alphabet in which symbols called letters represent sounds and can be grouped into words. Over the years, various peoples added and subtracted letters. For example, the letters J, V and W weren't invented until the Middle Ages.

Alphabets were invented fairly early in human history, but the tools used to write them down with are still being invented today. Long ago the kind of writing tools people used depended on the stuff they wrote on. For instance in the Middle East, early people wrote on clay tablets because there was lots of clay available. They cut hollow reed "pens" to press marks into the wet clay. When the clay tablet was filled with marks, it was baked until it was rock hard. Try erasing that!

The ancient Egyptians wrote on animal skins scraped thin, called parchment, or on papyrus, which was made by pressing and flattening the stems of the papyrus plant. To write on parchment or papyrus, they invented the fountain pen. Surprised? The earliest fountain pen – a reed into which ink could be poured – was found in a 6,000-year-old Egyptian tomb. But fountain pens as we know them weren't invented until the 1880s. Until then most people used quill pens made out of sharpened bird feathers and, later, nibbed pens dipped into ink.

Fountain pens had tiny tanks of ink inside them, so they didn't run out of ink as quickly as quill or nibbed pens. But they did have a drawback: the nibs would split or break and the ink would come splooshing out. It was easy to tell a fountain-pen-user by the ink stains on his or her clothes and fingers.

In the 1930s, several inventors started experimenting. Instead of nibs, they tried tiny balls that rolled the ink onto the paper. But no matter what they tried, none of the inventors could come up with a way to keep the ink in these "ball-point" pens running smoothly. It either clotted or blobbed.

A Hungarian named Ladislao Biro became interested in the problem. He had seen printers' inks at the newspaper where he worked and thought they might work. He began experimenting and continued to search for the perfect ink formula when he fled to Argentina during World War II. Finally, in 1944 – success! By using a rough ball and a new formula for ink, Biro's new ball-points worked beautifully. Biro started up a factory and began turning out pens. But after all that work, no one seemed to want them. Then an Englishman named Henry Martin spotted one of the pens. He thought they might be useful for wartime aircraft crews, who complained that their fountain pens leaked at high altitudes. Martin tested the new pens and the flight crews were enthusiastic. Soon ball-point pens were selling in the millions all over the world.

THE BOOK

The story of the pen doesn't end there. Although the ball-point pen solved aircraft crews' problems, it didn't solve astronauts' problems. Ordinary ball-point pens need gravity to help force the ink into contact with the ball. Up in space, there's no gravity, so the ink just won't come out in a smooth flow. Then an American named Paul Fisher invented the Fisher Space Pen. It has its own internal pressure source to hold the ink against the ball. And it also uses special "thixotropic" ink, which stays solid until the ball in the pen rubs against it. Then a bit of ink turns liquid.

American astronauts gave the Space Pen such rave reviews that today even the Soviet cosmonauts use it. Space Pens are also being sold right here on earth. Anyone can use them, but they're especially useful under water. Try one next time you get the urge to write in the bathtub.

The invention of the alphabet and writing tools in ancient times allowed people to write down knowledge and information. But what was needed was a way to pass that written-down information around. Clay tablets were heavy and cumbersome to pass around, and papyrus scrolls weren't much better. A flattened-out papyrus scroll could be as long as two school buses parked end to end. Finding something in the middle took a lot of rolling. Then someone (no one knows who) came up with the brilliant idea of cutting scrolls into chunks. Today we call them pages. When the pages were attached together at one edge, making a rough-looking book, it was easy to flick through them and find what you wanted.

Paper was invented by a Chinese courtier named Ts'ai Lun in the year 105. He found that by mashing up plants with water and spreading the mush over a screen, so that the water could drain off, you were left with a sheet of stuff you could write on. Later, shredded rags were used instead of plants. No one else knew about paper until some Chinese paper-makers were captured by Muslims in 751. From the Muslims paper-making gradually spread to Europe. Paper was much easier and cheaper to make than either papyrus or parchment, and it could be made in huge quantities so more and more books could be produced.

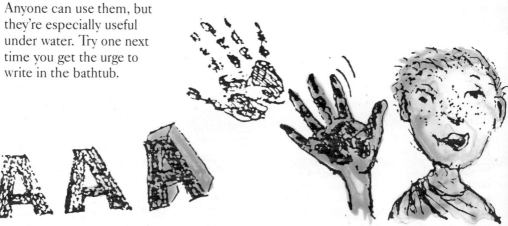

For hundreds of years books were written by hand, usually by scribes or monks. Sometimes monks would hand-paint elaborate designs and pictures into the text. A single book might take months or even years to hand-copy and illustrate. Printing changed all that. It was invented in China some time before the year 868. To print a page, someone would have to carve a wooden version of the page out of a large block of wood. Every word would have to be painstakingly carved out. But in 1041, a Peking blacksmith named Pi-Sheng invented a system of using tiny individual letters that could be arranged to form words to print one page, then rearranged to form new words for the next page. His idea of a printing press using "movable type" was later reinvented in Germany by Johann Gutenberg in about 1436. Nowadays billions of books roll off printing presses every year.

Before books were invented, information was slowly spread by one person learning from another. So, for example, if you wanted to know how to cure a sick pig, you had to travel to a neighboring healer and ask how. Then you had to trudge home and try it, hoping you hadn't forgotten anything. With a book, you didn't have to travel – or rely on your memory. You could look up what you wanted whenever you wanted.

As more and more books were written and printed, people had more and more information at their fingertips. This not only helped farmers with sick pigs; it spread information about science, medicine, nature, geography and other areas of knowledge. Books (and the information they contained) paved the way for many other inventions.

MONEY

Today, if you want to buy a pair of shoes, you simply walk into a store, pick out the pair you want and hand over the cash (or a cheque or a credit card) to pay for it. But 2,500 years ago, before money was invented, buying a pair of shoes or anything else was a big deal – literally.

Since you didn't have money, you'd have to barter something for the shoes – let's say a spare sheep.

First you would have to find someone with just the opposite problem – someone with a spare pair of shoes in need of a sheep. Now the trouble really begins. Since a sheep is worth more than a pair of shoes, the other person would have to give you the shoes plus, say, five chickens. If you didn't want the chickens, you could shop around and see if you could find a third person who'd give you something you *did* want for the chickens.

Whew! All that for a pair of shoes.

Then someone thousands of years ago invented the idea of money. Almost anything could be, and was, used as money: beads, shells, even fish hooks. In the area around Turkey, gold coins were used. At first, each coin was worth a different amount. Then in about 700 B.C., Gyges, the king of Lydia, invented the standard coin. It was issued under his name,

much the same way as today's coins are issued by governments.

Carrying a pouch full of coins made shopping a lot easier. While it could be difficult to find someone who wanted to barter your sheep for his shoes, it was easy to find someone who would sell a pair of shoes for coins. Everyone wanted coins. They allowed people to buy whatever they wished. But coins were still heavy and cumbersome – and

they attracted thieves. Greek and Roman traders who bought and sold goods with people in faraway cities invented cheques to stop robberies. A robber looking for gold and silver wasn't likely to be interested in a mere piece of paper that could be used only by the person whose name appeared on it. Then banks and some individuals began to issue pieces of paper in exchange for gold deposited with them. Anyone who had

one of these bank notes could use it like cash. Finally, about 300 years ago, governments began printing paper money.

Some strange things have been used as money over the years. Recently an irate American taxpayer, who claimed the tax department was taking everything he owned – even the shirt off his back – paid his tax bill with a cheque written on (what else) the shirt off his back.

COMPUTERS

Money made trade flourish. As more and more people bought and sold more and more things, abacuses were used to help with all the calculations that had to be done. The abacus was invented about 5,000 years ago, probably by the Babylonians who lived in the Middle East. Although it was extremely simple – just a series of wooden beads on rods – it was also extremely fast and accurate in the hands of a skilled user. Until the electronic calculator came along, an abacus could outperform any other calculator.

The abacus never caught on in Europe. There, some inventors created calculation machines, but none of them worked very well. Others put together mathematical tables, a bit like multiplication tables, to help speed up calculations. These tables, unfortunately, were filled with errors. And that drove an Englishman named Charles Babbage crazy.

Babbage liked things to be orderly and accurate. He was irritated by the mistakes he found in books of mathematical tables and frustrated by the amount of time it took to look up information in these cumbersome tables. He dreamed of inventing a machine that could do mathematical calculations fast and accurately. Starting in the 1820s, Babbage spent much of his time and money inventing such a machine. The result of all his labor was something he called "the Analytical Engine," which could be programmed to follow the instructions on a paper tape punched with holes. It was the first primitive computer.

Unfortunately, Babbage was ahead of his time. There was no electricity to make the machine work. The only source of power was steam. So the Analytical Engine never got past the model stage.

Babbage died a disappointed man in 1871, but others took up his work. They improved on his machine and added new ideas of their own. Some tried to perfect a calculating machine. Others wanted their machines to do more. They wanted machines that could take instructions, make decisions and do a variety of tasks in addition to calculations. Gradually their experiments paid off. During World War II, a British team built a computer that broke secret enemy codes and helped the Allies win the war. In America, calculator-computers helped with the 1880 census and with the operation of the telephone system.

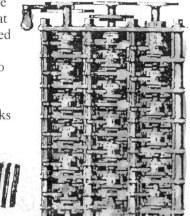

You wouldn't want one of these early calculator-computers on your desk. For example, the Mark I, built by a Harvard University team in 1943, measured 17 m (55 feet) long and 2.5 m (8 feet) high. Instead of the microchips that run today's computers, it had thousands of tiny tubes like the ones found in old radios.

The Mark I could multiply two 11-digit numbers in 3 seconds. Its successor, ENIAC (which stands for Electronic Numerical Integrator and Computer), cut that time to 3/1000 of a second. In the late 1940s, teams in Britain and the United States built electronic computers capable of storing a program, and the computer age was launched.

The speed and "intelligence" of the early computers surprised many people and spooked more than a few. People thought the computers could actually think for themselves. This idea was helped along by mischievous programmers, such as those at the University of Manitoba who programmed a computer to cheat at a guess-the-number game. Human players came away with the uncomfortable feeling that there was more to the computer than met the eye. Then there were movies like *2001: A Space Odyssey*, in which a computer named HAL, which has a mind of its own, decides to take over a space vehicle and kill off the astronauts.

Many of people's fears about computers were put to rest as computers became smaller (thanks to transistors) and more common. The first minicomputer was invented in 1963; it was the size of a fridge. Microchips and microprocessors "shrunk" computers even more.

Today computers are used in millions of homes, offices and factories. This book, for example, was written on a home computer, typeset on a computerized system and printed by a computer-driven printing press. Computers have already changed the world and are likely to change it even more in the future. One day you may find yourself using your home computer to call up a book you need for a project, help you word-process your project and then send it by modem to your teacher for marking. You might be able to order a new sweater from a store by computer and transfer money from your bank account to pay for it. And you might be able to use your home computer to program your own household robot.

ROBOTS

If the idea of a household robot seems far-fetched to you, you may be in for a surprise. A vacuuming robot was invented by a Japanese company called Automax in 1983, and robots may very well be an important part of the home of the future. Robots are already changing people's lives. There are more than 8,000 robots in the world doing the dirty, dangerous and boring work that once had to be done by humans.

Robots have been possible only since the invention of computers. But long before computers were around, people were fascinated by the idea of a machine that could mimic a human being.

Around the year 250 B.C., an inventor named Ctesibius is said to have built statues that could drink water. By the 1700s, many inventors were trying to create machines that would do even more. These were called automatons. One of the greatest automaton inventors was Pierre Jacquet-Droz. He made many elaborate moving figures, including one of a young boy who would dip his pen into an inkpot and write any 40-word sentence in either French or English. Another famous automaton was invented by Jacques de Vaucanson in 1738. It was a mechanical duck that could do everything a real duck can – eat grain, drink water, digest its food and even eliminate the waste. Of course it could quack and swim too.

Many of the early automatons were experiments to see how much machines could be made to do. Some were toys, usually for the sons and daughters of kings. Princes had automated toy soldiers and princesses had animated dolls. One Indian ruler even had a close-to-life-sized tiger that would attack a soldier.

The word "robot" was invented by a Czech writer named Karel Čapek in 1920. He wrote a play about robots that were supposed to improve life on earth but that ended by destroying it. A lot of people wrote stories or made movies about robots. Usually the robots could walk, talk and do everything humans could do. (In movies this was usually possible thanks to a human hiding inside.) And usually they were evil creatures who rebelled against their creators and ran amok.

In real life, robots were simple machines that couldn't walk or talk, let alone run amok. The invention of the computer changed all that. It gave robots brains. Although computer-equipped robots can't think, they can follow instructions. Robots work alongside humans on assembly lines, taking over some of the repetitive jobs. They handle hot or dangerous materials that might harm humans. And they lift and move

things that it would take many people to shift. They even go to places where humans cannot go. The Viking I Lander, one of the most sophisticated robots ever invented, walked on Mars in 1976, collecting samples, analyzing them and beaming the results back to scientists on Earth. Other robots go to ocean depths that would kill people. They send back pictures of wrecks, retrieve machinery and collect information about the ocean and its creatures.

Robots are active in other areas too. One robot named Aaron is a painter. Instructed by a human master, he turns out "slavepieces" (his master paints masterpieces).

A robot named Hero I once testified before a U.S. government committee. Hero's message? Robots are great. Another robot named Sim One looks and acts like a real hospital patient. It helps teach doctors how to cope with medical problems and can even simulate dying.

Although robots are far from human, inventors can't seem to resist giving them human names and capabilities. Robots have been named Roberta, BOB (stands for Brains on Board) and even Robot Redford.

Inventors are now working on ways to get robots to see things as we do, feel things and walk.

The more advanced robots become, the closer they come to science fiction. In 1983, for example, a factory was set up in Japan where robots manufacture – you guessed it – other robots!

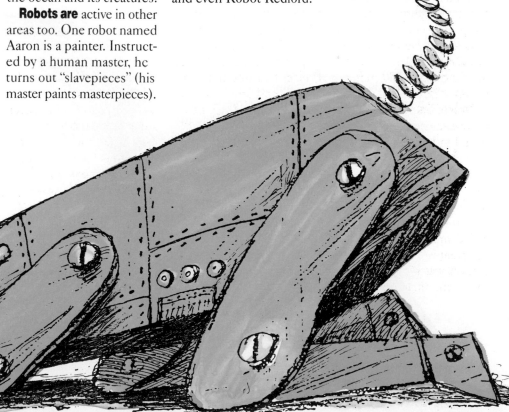

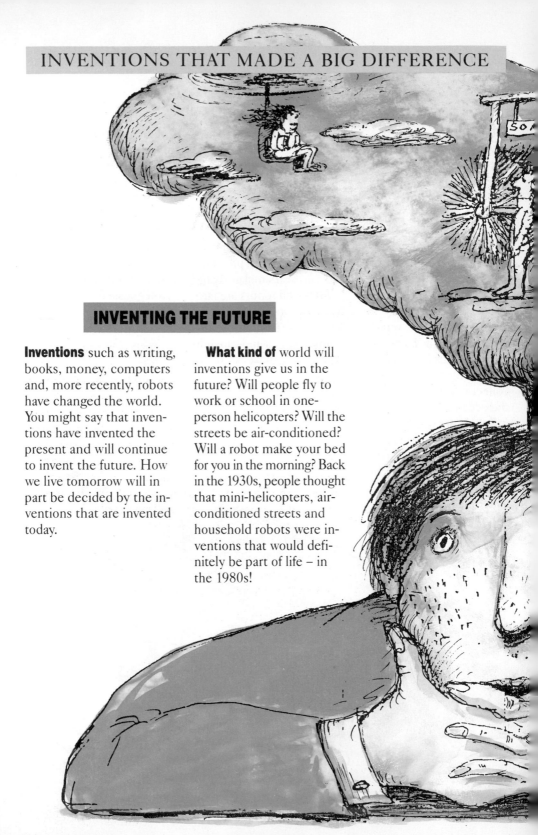

INVENTING THE FUTURE

Inventions such as writing, books, money, computers and, more recently, robots have changed the world. You might say that inventions have invented the present and will continue to invent the future. How we live tomorrow will in part be decided by the inventions that are invented today.

What kind of world will inventions give us in the future? Will people fly to work or school in one-person helicopters? Will the streets be air-conditioned? Will a robot make your bed for you in the morning? Back in the 1930s, people thought that mini-helicopters, air-conditioned streets and household robots were inventions that would definitely be part of life – in the 1980s!

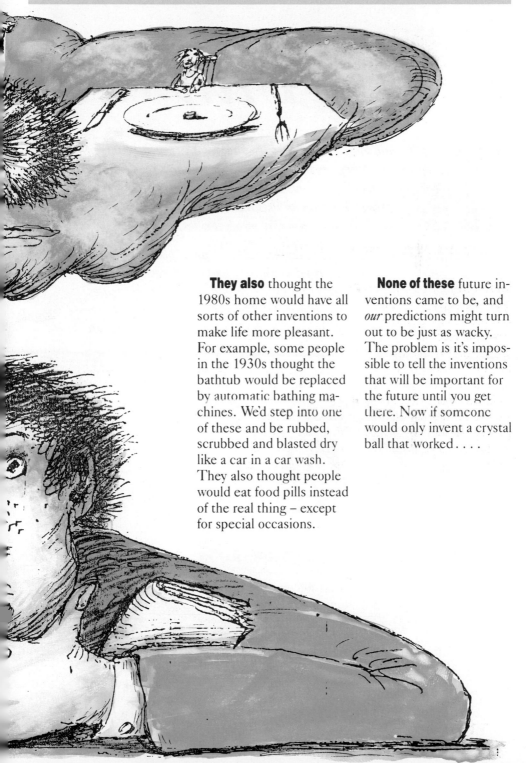

They also thought the 1980s home would have all sorts of other inventions to make life more pleasant. For example, some people in the 1930s thought the bathtub would be replaced by automatic bathing machines. We'd step into one of these and be rubbed, scrubbed and blasted dry like a car in a car wash. They also thought people would eat food pills instead of the real thing – except for special occasions.

None of these future inventions came to be, and *our* predictions might turn out to be just as wacky. The problem is it's impossible to tell the inventions that will be important for the future until you get there. Now if someone would only invent a crystal ball that worked. . . .

Fun and

While some inventors were changing the world by inventing such things as the alphabet, computers, television and electric lights, others were fooling around with toys and games. Their inventions didn't exactly revolutionize life on earth – but they sure made it a lot more fun.

TOYS AND GAMES have been around as long as people have. Archaeologists are no longer surprised when they find paintings of ancient Egyptians bowling or the remains of 3,000-year-old Norwegian ice skates. They've come to expect surprises. If you could take a trip back through time with them, here are a few of the inventions you'd find people dreaming up to make life a bit more fun.

10,500 YEARS AGO

Pets: You may not think of your dog or cat as an invention, but long ago people did invent *the idea* of keeping animals around the house. The first pets were wild dogs who crept near human campfires to eat leftover food scraps. Friendly dogs were allowed to stay, while unfriendly ones were chased off. Early dogs may have acted as guard dogs. They woofed when wild animals or other people approached. But gradually they came to be part of the family, mooching food and snuggling up at night with their masters the way dogs do today.

Games

Over thousands of years new breeds of pet dogs were "invented" by man. Some were long and low-slung (dachshunds), others were hairy (Samoyeds), still others were good at pulling (huskies) or running (greyhounds). Few of these breeds would have survived without human protection. Out in the wild, they probably would have perished.

Since the "invention" of the pet dog, many other animals have become pets too, including cheetahs, turtles, baboons and mongooses. The Roman emperor Caligula is even said to have had a pet lion, which liked to attend the emperor's banquets. Having a lion sitting next to you would certainly make you mind your manners, wouldn't it?

As time passed, pets became more and more pampered. Special pet foods and toys were invented to feed and amuse them, and some animal lovers even came up with animal clothes. Although there are rubber boots for dogs and coats for cats, so far no one has come up with anything suit-able for fish.

MORE THAN 6,000 YEARS AGO

Dolls: Dolls made out of clay have been found in ancient ruins from about 4000 B.C. But dolls were probably invented long before that. Their inventor was probably a child who lived many thousands of years ago.

Dolls have changed a lot over the years. They have been made out of china, porcelain, wax and papier-mâché. They have been designed to burp, wet their pants, cry, wiggle, kiss, play pat-a-cake, walk, talk and even wash their own hair.

Some famous inventors have tried their hands at inventing dolls. Thomas

Edison, who invented the phonograph, also thought up – what else – a phonographic doll. It looked like an ordinary doll, but if you removed a panel in the body you could see a miniature phonograph. Like Edison's real phonograph (see page 51), the phonographic doll could both record sounds and play them back. It was sort of like a tape recorder with legs.

Another famous inventor, Orville Wright, also invented a doll. Wright is best known as the person who made the first successful airplane flight, in 1903. Twenty years later, it seems he was still hooked on flight. He invented a flying doll. It didn't have wings. Instead it was shot through the air with the help of a spring, did a flying somersault and grabbed onto a wire.

One of the most famous dolls of all is the Barbie doll. Although now around age 30 (she was invented in 1958 by Mattel), Barbie still looks as young as ever. She has a big family and an even bigger wardrobe. To date, more Barbies and Barbie family members have been manufactured than there are people in the entire United States.

73

A THOUSAND YEARS AGO

Playing Cards: The first playing cards were invented by the Chinese around the year 986. They were much longer and narrower than today's cards and were decorated to look like paper money of the time.

At first, playing cards had a bad reputation. One Chinese emperor told of a duke who had played cards. He had been killed and all his subjects had "become victims of barbarity." The emperor believed that card-playing brought on these misfortunes. But despite the bad associations, cards had spread to Europe by the 1200s.

The first card games were probably a lot like the modern game of Snap; high cards captured lower ones. Our modern deck of cards developed over hundreds of years. At times as many

as 78 cards made up a pack, instead of our 52. And different countries had different suits. (The modern deck has four suits: spades, hearts, diamonds and clubs.) In Germany, for example, people played with hearts, bells, leaves and acorns; in Italy, with swords, batons, cups and money.

People often gambled with cards to make money. In early Canada cards once served as money. Cards came to be used because a

ship containing soldiers' wages was delayed and the soldiers wanted to be paid. The governor of New France (now part of Canada) gave them playing cards instead. Each was worth a certain amount of money and was signed by the governor as a guarantee. Although playing-card money was supposed to be a temporary solution, it lasted for 70 years.

225 YEARS AGO

Roller Skates: Roller skates were a smash hit right from the start. To demonstrate the first pair in 1760, their inventor, a Belgian musician named Joseph Merlin, made a spectacular entrance to a British ball. Playing the violin as he skated, Merlin shot onto the dance floor. Alas, the skates had no brakes. Merlin whooshed past stunned onlookers and crashed into a huge mirror.

Merlin started a new fad. Soon hundreds of roller skaters were slamming into one another, bouncing off trees and lamp posts and skinning knees and hands as they went down.

Merlin's roller skates had two large wheels each. Other roller skate inventors added and subtracted wheels, trying to find a roller skate that was both maneuverable *and* stable. Some had as many as five wheels; others as few as one. Wearing some, you could only skate in straight lines; others wanted to keep turning. In 1863 an American named James Plimpton invented the four-wheelers that you use today.

115 YEARS AGO

Chewing Gum: Next time someone complains about your gum chewing, say you're exercising your jaw. That's why chewing gum was invented when it was patented by an Ohio dentist, William Semple, in 1869. Semple's chewing gum never caught on as a jaw exerciser. Instead people preferred to chew flavorful gum from the spruce tree. Unfortunately, this "spruce gum" became hard to find as newspapers grew and ate up all the spruce trees for paper.

About the same time as the Ohio dentist patented his jaw-exercising gum, a relative of two U.S. presidents by the name of Thomas Adams learned about a new kind of rubber called chicle. Chicle is the rubbery sap of the sapodilla tree, which grows in parts of Central America. Adams believed that chicle could be a revolutionary new material, if only he could find a way to vulcanize it the way Charles Goodyear had vulcanized rubber. But no matter what Adams did, chicle wouldn't stretch or bounce or do anything else useful.

One day while in a drug-store, Adams overheard a young girl asking for some chewing gum. Adams remembered that he had heard of South American Indians chewing chicle. He talked the store-owner into trying chicle formed into balls. Gum-chewing kids loved it, and it solved the problem of the spruce gum shortage. In 1871 Adams invented a machine that rolled the chicle gum into sticks, and he put some flavor into it for the first time since spruce gum. Before long all of America was chewing this chicle

gum that was, Adams claimed, "health-giving, circulation-building, teeth-preserving, digestion-aiding, brain-refreshing, chest-developing, nerve-settling and soul-tuning." Not bad for a stick of gum.

New gum inventions were soon on the way. Small chunks of gum were coated with candy and called little chicles, or Chiclets. When you bit into one, the candy coating squished into the flavorless gum inside. Extra-strong gum that could be blown into bubbles followed. The early stuff was called Blibber-Blubber, and when it popped you practically needed turpentine to get it off your face.

By the 1950s, people around the world were chewing gum. In Japan, for example, people chewed gum flavored to resemble green tea and pickled plums. Gum was even chewed by astronauts in space. The first gum chewing in space took place on the American Gemini 5 mission in 1965. At least that's the official version. However, some people believe gum was smuggled aboard an earlier space flight. How did the astronauts get rid of the smuggled gum when they came back to Earth? They did what thousands of school kids have done over the years when caught with gum: they swallowed it.

95 YEARS AGO

Basketball: When a Canadian named James Naismith invented a new game in 1891, his friends tried to persuade him to call it Naismithball. Fortunately he was too modest and decided to call it basketball instead. Naismith was a phys-ed instructor at the Young Men's Christian Association Training School in Springfield, Massachusetts, when he was struck by the need for a good indoor team game. Cold weather made playing outdoors impossible, and games such as baseball and football required too much space to be played indoors. So Naismith set out to invent a game that would combine the most exciting parts of several outdoor games and that could be played in a gymnasium.

The game he came up with called for two teams who tried to score points by getting a large, light-weight ball into a basket mounted high up on the wall. For the first game, two peach baskets were borrowed from the school janitor to serve as goals. To make the game challenging and playable on an indoor court, he outlawed running with the ball except while bouncing it. And because it was played on a hard floor, he didn't allow tackling.

Naismith's students loved the new game – even though it did have some problems. For instance, there was the overcrowding problem. Teams were huge – some had as many as 50 players.

That meant a lot of jostling and bumping. And then there was the basket problem. When a team scored a point, the ball sat in the basket and everyone had to wait around until someone got a ladder to get it down. Gradually these problems were worked out. Teams were limited to five players and a hole was cut in the bottom of the bushel basket so that the ball would fall right through. In 1906, hoops with bottomless nets took the place of the baskets.

Recently historians have uncovered information about a game very much like basketball played by the Aztecs of Central America several hundred years ago. Called *ollamalitzli,* it was played by shooting a solid rubber ball through a stone hoop. It seems that scoring must have been very difficult. According to the rules, any player who managed to score could claim as a reward the clothes of all the spectators.

25 YEARS AGO

Skateboarding: When Greg Molenaar of Washington goes to work, people stop to watch. Why? Molenaar rides to work on a motorized skateboard that he invented. Although the skateboard won't set any speed records (just as well, since it doesn't have any brakes), it does get excellent gas mileage – about 1.2L/100 km (200 miles per gallon).

Molenaar's motorized version is one recent improvement to the skateboard, which was invented in the early 1960s. No one knows exactly who invented the skateboard. Probably a California surfer, frustrated by poor surfing conditions, decided to attach a miniature version of a surfboard to a pair of roller skates and try "surfing" on dry land. By 1965, everyone was skateboarding. . .and having accidents. It seems that the wheels on early skateboards, borrowed from roller skates, were just too hard and smooth. They didn't give a skateboarder any traction. As a result skateboarders had even more accidents than bicyclists. To squelch this dangerous new sport, several North American cities banned skateboarding on streets and sidewalks.

But skateboarding was just too much fun to be abandoned. In 1973 Frank Nasworthy invented a new plastic-like wheel covering that gave better traction and skateboarding took off again. Special skateboarding parks were built and competitions held. Moves such as tic-tacking, ro-los, daffys and powerslides were invented to test skateboarders' skills. And names like road rash and pavement pizza were invented to describe the skin burns and scabs you ended up with if you weren't lucky. However, despite the danger, the skateboard was here to stay.

TODAY AND YESTERDAY

Today Space Age technology is revolutionizing an ancient game: bowling. The ancient Egyptians first played it about 7,200 years ago by bowling a stone ball down a lane and through three hoops and knocking down stone pins. The ancient Egyptians would be astounded by modern bowling alleys with their computerized scoring aids. And they'd probably be delighted with the latest improvements in bowling balls.

Instead of being cut from chunks of stone, as the Egyptian balls were, today's bowling balls are made out of a liquid plastic that is poured into a mold and left to harden. The perfect bowling ball should be a bit top-heavy. But finding the heavy spot – and therefore the top of the ball, where the finger holes should go – has long been a problem for bowling-ball-makers. Then one company asked the National Aeronautics and Space Administration (NASA) for help.

NASA recommended using a weighing system that had been developed for the Voyager space program. A bowling ball was floated in a special bath, where it rolled until the heaviest part faced down. Then a marking device marked the heavy spot and the finger holes could be drilled. The new process, called Exactatron, has brought a 7,200-year-old game into the Space Age.

The Inventive Mind

f you think of inventors as wild-haired, absentminded scientists surrounded by bottles, wires and bits and pieces of bizarre inventions, you're not alone. That's how inventors have been portrayed in books such as Frankenstein *and movies like* Back to the Future. *But are inventors really forgetful (sometimes slightly mad) geniuses? What makes an inventor? And what makes an inventor invent? Let's take a peek into the inventive mind to find out.*

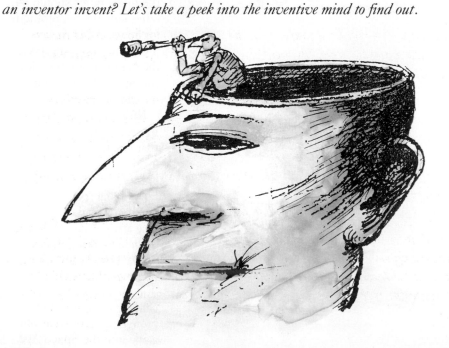

THE FIRST THING *you'd notice if you could shrink and climb into an inventor's brain is that it looks pretty much like anyone else's. It's no bigger than ordinary and there's no special drawer marked "inventive genius." A quick look into the drawer marked "education" might surprise you though, especially if you expect inventors to be academic whizzes. Some inventors, including Orville and Wilbur Wright, never made it through high school. Percy Spencer, who invented the microwave oven, only got as far as fifth grade, yet he received about 250 patents for his inventions over his lifetime.*

THE DRAWER MARKED *"experience" might also be a bit of a shocker. Although many chemists invent chemicals and many farmers invent new farm tools, some inventors have come up with things that have nothing to do with their usual line of work. Try matching the inventors on the left with the correct invention on the right:*

a veterinarian	*parking meter*
a traveling salesman	*air-filled bicycle tire*
a newspaperman	*safety razor*

You're right if you guessed that a veterinarian invented the air-filled bicycle tire, a traveling salesman invented the safety razor and a newspaperman invented the parking meter.

BUT THE INVENTIVE *mind does have some special qualities. It's curious and willing to follow an idea no matter where it leads. And it's tenacious – it doesn't give up easily. Some inventors have so much curiosity and tenacity that they seem a little bit odd to the rest of us. They concentrate on inventing, not on day-to-day life. Perhaps that's why they are thought of as absentminded.*

JUST ABOUT *everyone has some inventiveness tucked away in the back of his or her mind. And everyone seems to have a different approach to inventing too. Take the bicycle, for example. It seems a simple enough thing, doesn't it? All you need is two wheels, gears, pedals, a seat and handlebars to steer with. If that's how you think of bicycles, you're in for a surprise.*

THE INVENTIVE MIND TACKLES THE BICYCLE

As long ago as 1200 B.C. an inventive Egyptian realized that having a pair of wheels would be a faster and easier way of getting around than walking. A drawing found in an Egyptian tomb shows a two-wheeled vehicle that the rider probably moved by pushing his feet against the ground. The idea seems to have disappeared for many years, until a German, Baron Carl von Drais von Sauerbronn, reinvented it in 1817. His "dandy horse," a two-wheeler without pedals, was all the rage among rich Parisians and soon caught on in England, where it was called the hobbyhorse.

Pedals were finally added to the two-wheeler by a Scottish blacksmith named Kirkpatrick Macmillan in 1839. His pedals didn't go in circles as pedals do on modern bicycles; they went back and forth. Modern-style pedals were added in 1885, and air-filled tires were invented in 1888 by Belfast veterinarian John Dunlop.

You might expect the story of the bicycle to end with the two-wheeler. But it didn't. Inventive minds in various parts of the world fell in love with the idea of pedal-powered cycles, and before long there were hundreds of new bicycle inventions, each stranger than the last.

Some bicycle inventors started on the wheels. If two wheels were good, why not three or even more?

And why not wheels of various sizes? Some cycles had one enormous wheel. Others had two huge wheels or one large and two small wheels. People riding these giant three-wheelers looked like overgrown toddlers.

Other inventors concentrated on the source of power – the rider, or riders. Various inventors came up with bicycles built for two, three, even whole families.

However, the most unusual bicycle inventions were never used on the roads. They were designed for air or water. Inventors glued on wings and tried to pedal their way skyward. Or they cut holes in the bottom of boats and inserted bicycles to make watercycles. Most of the watercycles were designed for paddling around parks. But the aircycles were serious business. They were a creative attempt to solve a problem that faced early aircraft inventors: the need for a lightweight source of power. At the time the only power source available was the steam engine, which was far too big and heavy for airplanes. When small gasoline engines finally became available in the early 1900s, the Wright brothers were quick to use them and most inventors lost interest in pedal-powered flight – except, as we have seen, inventors of human-powered planes (see page 17).

Fewer inventors have tackled the bicycle in the last hundred years. But some just couldn't resist fiddling. A British inventor came up with a solar-powered bicycle. It's great for sunny days, but when the clouds come, get ready to pedal. And a 16-year-old Canadian named Gilles Lablond invented a water tricycle by attaching truck inner tubes to a 10-speed. Because there's very little friction between the tires and the water, the Lablondmobile isn't likely to set any speed records. But it does prove that getting there is half the fun. Speed records are being set, however, by another new bicycle design, which the rider pedals while lying on his or her back. It's called the Lightning X2, for good reason. It can reach speeds of up to 92 km/h (58 miles per hour).

For most people, the bicycle was a handy way of getting from place to place. For inventive minds it was just a starting point. They took the idea of the bicycle and fiddled, stretched, twisted, tinkered and played with it.

AHEAD OF THEIR TIMES

Inventive minds sometimes get a bit carried away in their search for new ideas. They might come up with a great-sounding idea, such as attaching a helicopter blade to a bicycle, but the resulting aerial cycle just won't fly. Some inventions are truly far-fetched. But others are just ahead of their time; they don't work because they need materials or power sources or machinery that don't yet exist. Today an aerial cycle might sound silly, but in 50 years... who knows? Maybe your grandchildren will be cycling around overhead.

All through history inventive minds have dreamed up inventions that are too far ahead of their time to be workable. In 6th-century China, for example, someone came up with the idea of attaching sails to wooden carts. The resulting contraption looked like a pioneer wagon with a sail and could hold as many as 30 people. These "landboats" never caught on – until the 1920s. That's when iceboat racers discovered that they could have fun all year round by attaching wheels to their iceboats and racing them in summer.

Lots of people have predicted inventions that are hundreds of years in the future. In the year 1260, Friar Roger Bacon predicted the day when "wagons may be built which will move with incredible speed and without the aid of beasts." The idea of horseless carriages was scorned for hundreds of years until, in 1771, a French engineer named Nicolas Cugnot built a three-wheeled steam-driven car. Even Cugnot was ahead of his time. Before an efficient car could be invented, more compact engines had to be

developed. The first gaso-line-powered car was invented in 1885 by a German named Karl Benz. It could coast along at speeds of up to – hold on to your hat – 13 km/h (8 miles per hour).

One inventor who was hundreds of years ahead of his time was Leonardo da Vinci. Today he is best known as a painter of masterpieces, but he also invented everything from flying machines and parachutes to horseless wagons. He drew pictures of his inventions and recorded his ideas in backwards writing, perhaps to keep others from stealing them. His inventions are startlingly like the machines we have today. However, few of them made it past the idea stage, usually because they were so far ahead of their time that it

would have been impossible to build them with the materials then available.

Leonardo also had a playful streak. He invented an alarm clock, which he described like this: "When as much water has been poured through the funnel into the receiver as there is in the opposite balance, this balance rises and pours its water into the first receiver; and this being doubled in weight jerks violently upwards the foot of the sleeper, who is thus awakened and goes to his work." Now that's a rude awakening.

FOR THE FUN OF IT

Fun is often an important part of inventing. Inventors can't resist seeing what will happen when they connect two ideas or two things that normally aren't connected. Sometimes the results are pretty silly. For example, in 1954 an American company came up with something called a Floater Bubble. It combined an inner tube with hip waders. The idea was that people going fishing could wade into lakes or streams and, if necessary, swim after their catch. The fisherman wearing a Floater Bubble looked a bit like a rhinoceros in a ballerina's tutu – and was just about as awkward.

Then there was the bed-piano. The idea of combining a bed and a piano might seem rather odd to you, but it wasn't to Charles Hess. He even threw in a chest of drawers just to see what would happen. Although the bed-piano would be ideal for music lovers who suffer from insomnia, there is no record of one ever being built.

To a playful inventive mind, even something as serious as a life preserver could be a lot of fun. One had a wet suit and helmet to keep the wearer warm and dry, plus an attention-getting flag to signal rescuers. But the inventor didn't stop there. The life preserver also came equipped with a newspaper and cigar holder to keep the wearer happy while awaiting rescue. Unlike many silly inventions that never make it off the drawing board, this one was actually tested in the Hudson River.

Many people who invent for the fun of it have come up with new ways of getting from place to place. An inventor named William Richardson even thought up a way to improve swimming. In 1880 he invented a swimming machine that could help a swimmer reach breakneck speeds of 6 to 9 km/h (4 to 6 miles per hour) by furiously pedaling foot and hand cranks.

FAME?

Some people work on inventions hoping to become famous. Usually they don't. Even famous people sometimes have a tough time becoming famous for their inventions. Although Mark Twain invented a new kind of waistband and a self-pasting scrapbook, he's better known for writing such classics as *The Adventures of Huckleberry Finn*. Before becoming president of the United States, Abraham Lincoln invented air tanks to help float boats over river shallows. His invention never made him famous either. In fact, inventors are more likely to be forgotten than remembered. For example, who remembers Edwin Budding? Here's a hint: without his invention, you'd have to chop off the grass in your yard with a sickle or turn loose a flock of hungry sheep. Yes, he invented the lawn mower, in 1830.

You've probably never heard of the American inventor William Painter either, but you've used his invention. Painter had a string of successful inventions behind him when he turned his attention to making a better bottle cap in 1880. Before he came along, bottles were sealed with glass stoppers that were wired onto the bottle necks. You needed at least two hands – sometimes more – to remove one. These stoppers were not only awkward, they were also very expensive.

You might think a bottle cap is a simple thing – something an inventor could come up with in a week or so. But it took William Painter 11 years to invent a cheap cap that would completely seal a bottle. Today his invention, the flip-off crown cap, tops billions of pop bottles a year.

Painter's invention didn't change the world. But by discovering a cheap and easy way to seal bottles, he did help to speed the spread of soft drinks.

Another little-known inventor put color into people's lives. Try to imagine wearing only a few colors of clothes – red, brown, purple, black, gray or blue. That's the choice you would have had before 1856. Until then dyes used to tint cloth were made by crushing and boiling berries and other plants. It was impossible to make large quantities of green, orange and yellow dyes from plants, so only the wealthy could afford to have clothes in these colors. Then an 18-year-old Englishman named William Perkins had a happy accident.

Perkins was the young assistant to a scientist who was trying to make the anti-malaria drug quinine out of chemicals. During the Easter vacation of 1856, while experimenting in his backyard laboratory, he produced a thick reddish-brown sludge. Perkins was disappointed; the sludge wasn't quinine. So he substituted a few chemicals and tried again. This time he got black sludge. Most people would have thrown the sludge out, but not Perkins. He tried adding water to it and was astonished by the results. The water turned a beautiful mauve color.

It didn't take long for Perkins to realize that he had invented the first chemical dye. Soon everyone, including Queen Victoria, was wearing mauve clothes dyed with Perkins's happy accident. Within a few years clothes began appearing in a rainbow of new chemical colors.

A no less "colorful" unsung hero was Margaret Knight. She was a born inventor. At age 12 she saw a weaver injured when his shuttle flew off the loom and gashed him. Her first invention was a device that stopped the shuttle from leaving the loom.

During her long and inventive life, Knight invented close to 30 tools and machines. But perhaps her most famous was a machine to make flat-bottomed paper bags. No one knows who first thought up the paper bag. But until Knight invented a bag-making machine in 1867, those bags couldn't hold much. A flat bottom made bags easier to fill and allowed them to hold twice as much.

Unsung heroes such as Painter, Perkins and Knight have helped make life easier and more pleasant for the rest of us. Their inventions never made them famous, but it's difficult to imagine life without them. A few inventors, however, *do* become famous for inventing. Clarence Birdseye (page 37) and Charles Macintosh (page 30) even had their inventions named after them.

CHAPTER EIGHT

IN SEARCH OF SOMETHING BETTER

Many people become inventors because they are searching for something faster, hotter, prettier, softer, greener, sturdier, cooler, smaller, dryer, safer, lighter . . . in short, something better than what existed before.

Two American brothers, Lewis Barton and Curtis Lawson, turned their minds to inventing because they were tired of cleaning their family car. Their mother traveled a lot and ate at takeout restaurants. Food was always sliding off the takeout trays and onto the floor and seats of the car, where Lewis and Curtis had to clean it up. The two brothers decided to clean up the clean-up problem once and for all by inventing a spill-proof takeout tray with a built-in cupholder. Next the brothers tackled cleaning their swimming pool. They invented a fountain-like leaf pusher. It forces leaves and other pool garbage into a corner so that it can easily be scooped out.

Lewis and Curtis became inventors because they wanted to find easier and better ways to do things. Their inventions were so simple yet impressive that they were given the National Inventors Award in the U.S. in 1982. Lewis was 9 years old at the time, and Curtis was 13. Surprised? You shouldn't be – kids can be inventors too.

YOUNG INVENTORS

One of the youngest inventors ever to be awarded a patent was an American named Buddy Patch. He invented a toy truck in 1963 and got a patent for it when he was 6. Toys aren't the only inventions that kids have come up with.

In 1873, 15-year-old Chester Greenwood of Maine got tired of freezing his ears every time he went skating. A lot of kids would have just stayed inside and waited for spring, but Chester wasn't about to give up. He twisted some wire to fit over his head and asked his grandmother to sew on some bits of beaver fur at ear level. The result: the world's first earmuffs.

Another 15-year-old, Armand Bombardier, invented a new way of getting around in winter. Armand's home town of Valcourt, Quebec, got so much snow in winter that traveling by car was sometimes impossible. Armand attached a car motor to the family's sleigh. An old airplane propeller whirled around on the back of the contraption to help things along. Armand's neighbors were dumbfounded by the odd-looking motorized sleigh, but they gradually became used to it. Over the next few years Armand improved on his invention and dropped the propeller, finally patenting it in 1937. At first he thought he'd call his invention the ski-dog; today we call it the snowmobile.

Some young inventors go on to become famous when they grow up. One rising young inventor was Raymond Kurzweil. In 1960, at age 12, Kurzweil invented a computer program that could do in a few days the work that had once taken five people several weeks. A year later he invented a huge computer memory that could store 4,000 facts. And at 16, he invented a computer that could "listen" to one song and compose another very similar song. The machine that Kurzweil is famous for, though, could read this book. It scans the printed page, recognizes the words and speaks them out loud in a clear, robot-like voice. The Kurzweil Reading Machine, invented by Raymond Kurzweil when he was in his 20s, has made it possible for blind people to "read" anything they choose, without waiting for it to be translated into Braille.

CAN YOU BE AN INVENTOR?

When a national inventor's contest for kids was announced in the U.S. in 1985, 80,000 budding inventors sent in their ideas. One of the youngest, 5-year-old Katie Harding, invented an umbrella equipped with a flashlight so that her older brother could spot and side-step mud puddles in the dark. Third-grader Nicholas Goodman figured out a way to tame your hair in the morning, when it's been slept on the wrong way.

He invented a comb that sprays water as you use it. Fourteen-year-old Jim Wollin came up with a jar that could be opened at both ends. Why? So that you can get to the last bit of food hiding in the bottom. He called his invention "the jar of plenty."

You may have already invented something. If not, it's not too late to start. Although it seems that the world is already filled with inventions, there are still thousands of gadgets, tools, toys, materials, computer programs, plants, cars, robots and other things waiting to be invented. Ironically, some of the most needed inventions in the future will be pollution fighters designed to clean up the mess left by the inventions of the past.

What else is in store for the future of inventions? Will inventions extend our reach into space? Will they give us new ways to feed the world's growing population or help us explore the world inside the human body? It is you and others of your generation who will decide. After all, you are the inventors of the future.

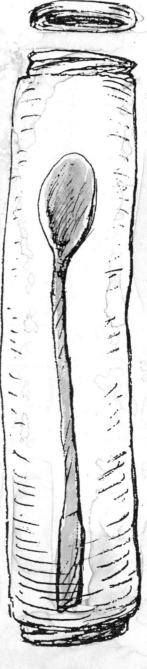

Index